SCHOOL OF AMERICAN RESEARCH PRESS

ARROYO HONDO ARCHAEOLOGICAL SERIES

DOUGLAS W. SCHWARTZ
GENERAL EDITOR

ARROYO HONDO ARCHAEOLOGICAL SERIES

1
The Contemporary Ecology of
Arroyo Hondo, New Mexico
N. Edmund Kelley

2
Prehistoric Pueblo Settlement Patterns:
The Arroyo Hondo, New Mexico, Site Survey
D. Bruce Dickson, Jr.

3
Pueblo Population and Society:
The Arroyo Hondo Skeletal and Mortuary Remains
Ann M. Palkovich

ARROYO HONDO SKELETAL AND
MORTUARY REMAINS

The publication of this volume
was made possible by a grant from the
NATIONAL SCIENCE FOUNDATION.

PUEBLO POPULATION AND SOCIETY:

THE ARROYO HONDO SKELETAL AND MORTUARY REMAINS

Ann M. Palkovich

With an Appendix by James Mackey

SCHOOL OF AMERICAN RESEARCH PRESS
ARROYO HONDO ARCHAEOLOGICAL SERIES, Volume 3

SCHOOL OF AMERICAN RESEARCH PRESS
Post Office Box 2188
Santa Fe, New Mexico 87501

Douglas W. Schwartz, *General Editor*
Phillip Brittenham, *Director of Publications*
Jane Kepp, *Series Editor*

Library of Congress Cataloging in Publication Data

Palkovich, Ann M.
  Pueblo population and society.

  (Arroyo Hondo archaeological series; v. 3)
  Bibliography: p. 183
          1. Arroyo Hondo site, N.M.   2. Pueblo Indians
—Mortuary customs.   3. Indians of North America
—New Mexico—Mortuary customs.   I.   Title.
II.   Series.
E99.P9P27   978.9′53   80-51310
ISBN 0-933452-03-9

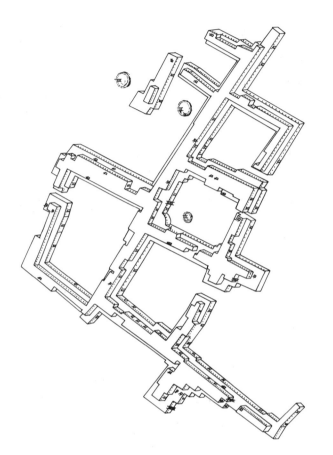

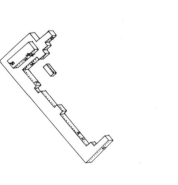

FIG. 1. Reconstruction of Arroyo Hondo Pueblo at its greatest size, about A.D. 1330.

Foreword

THE ARROYO HONDO PROJECT

Douglas W. Schwartz

At the peak of its population, Arroyo Hondo Pueblo was an impressive settlement composed of 1,000 rooms clustered symmetrically around ten plazas and housing well over a thousand people (Fig. 1). An arm of the southern Rocky Mountains served as a backdrop for the pueblo on the east, and to the south and west there were unobstructed views over grasslands to distant mountains. The town's active life lasted slightly more than a century, encompassing two separate episodes of rapid growth, each followed by precipitous decline. To understand both its dynamic and its transitory nature, Arroyo Hondo must be seen from two perspectives: externally, as part of a centuries-long expansion and contraction of agricultural villages in response to climate change in the northern Rio Grande region and, internally, in terms of its own life history.

The earliest clearly identifiable farming settlements in the northern Rio Grande valley date to the seventh century A.D., when average yearly precipitation began to increase and for several hundred years remained highly favorable for farming in this high, mountain-bordered valley (Karlstrom and Dean 1979:1,094). At first, settlements were located near the floodplains of permanent water courses best suited for early agricultural technology. But interrelated increases in agricultural yields and population size soon led to the expansion of villages within the valley and onto the higher, adjacent piedmont. As climatic conditions improved, what had been substandard land became agriculturally productive. With growth in the regional population, settlements appeared progressively farther from the rivers on land previously of secondary and marginal quality (Dickson 1980).

The greatest extent of Pueblo occupation came at the beginning of the fourteenth century, exemplified by Arroyo Hondo Pueblo and other towns built far from the major water courses. However, during that century, the long period of optimal precipitation came to an end, and by the early 1400s agricultural productivity had fallen dramatically. Arroyo Hondo was abandoned along with many other villages on what were then the edges of Pueblo territory. The limits of settlement in the northern Rio Grande region began to move back toward their earlier locations, reversing the order of their original expansion. Finally, the only remaining communities were those on the relatively permanent water courses, where they were discovered by the sixteenth-century Spanish explorers (Map 1).

ARROYO HONDO PUEBLO

Seen from a regional perspective, Arroyo Hondo Pueblo emerges as just one element in a greater pattern. Yet when viewed in terms of its own life history, the pueblo provides an example of human response on a smaller scale to the same forces that shaped the regional pattern of change. The town was founded about A.D. 1300, when a small group of settlers constructed an alignment of rooms along the edge of the Arroyo Hondo four and a half miles south of present-day Santa Fe, New Mexico. The location selected was on a gently sloping piedmont at an elevation of 7,100 feet, immediately west of the foothills of the Sangre de Cristo Mountains, which rise abruptly to nearly 12,000 feet. Emerging from the mountains and running southwest, the Arroyo Hondo cuts a gorge 125 feet deep through the alluvium and underlying rock. In the canyon below the pueblo was a free-flowing spring and

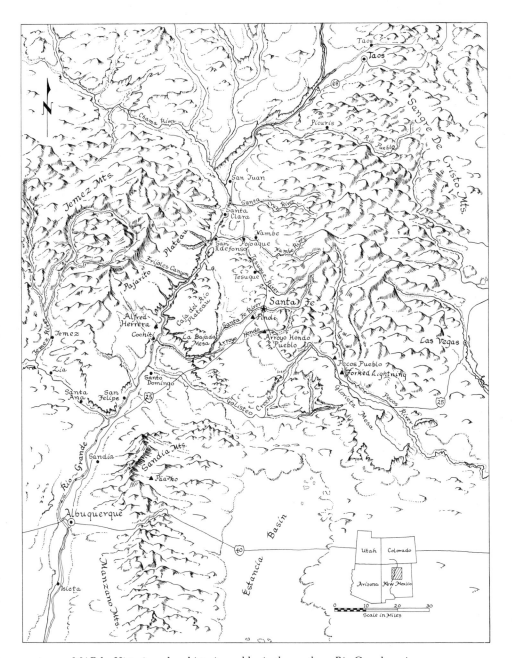

MAP 1. Historic and prehistoric pueblos in the northern Rio Grande region.

the best-watered soils of the area (Kelley 1980). The site of the pueblo, in the past as at present, was surrounded by a piñon-juniper woodland that graded into ponderosa pine toward the mountains and into grasslands as the elevation dropped toward the south and west (Fig. 2). Thus, the settlers had ready access to the combined plant and animal resources of several ecological zones.

From the start, the basis of the pueblo's economy was agriculture. At times, rainfall in the uplands around the settlement was sufficient to make dry farming productive, but this agricultural method produced highly variable results because of large fluctuations in yearly precipitation. The farmlands in the arroyo, however, offered good agricultural potential and greater reliability because they could support irrigation or floodwater farming. In the arroyo the settlers probably planted the first fields of corn, beans, and squash, crops supplemented by seasonally available wild greens, seeds, and nuts. Added protein was supplied by domesticated turkeys and at least fifty species of wild game, including jackrabbits, cottontails, mule deer, pronghorn antelope, and elk.

With this excellent ecological base and favorable climatic conditions, the pueblo grew to nearly a hundred times its original size in the first three decades of the 1300s. Adobe roomblocks were built at right angles to one another, forming great, open plazas that could be entered only by a single passageway. By 1310, the core rooms of seven roomblocks had been built, surrounding two plazas (Fig. 3). Within another ten years, the pueblo had expanded south and west, with eight new roomblocks partially enclosing two additional plazas. The settlement reached its greatest size around 1330, comprising 24 roomblocks constructed around ten wholly or partially enclosed plazas (Fig. 3). The population concentrated at the town by this time made Arroyo Hondo one of the larger communities in the region.

The roomblocks that composed the pueblo ranged from two to five rooms wide and up to fifteen rooms long. They were usually a single story along the exterior wall, stepping up to two stories near the central core. Internally, each block was divided into apartmentlike residence units of four or five interconnected ground-story rooms with related rooms on the second story. Rooms averaged about five square meters in floor area, were generally entered through the roof, and were used either for storage or as living quarters. In the latter case, they usually contained hearths and mealing bins. Rooftops and plaza surfaces served as important adjuncts to the rooms, being used for cooking, food

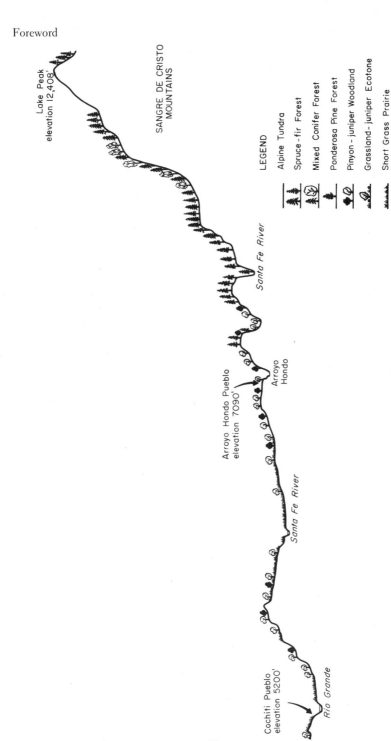

FIG. 2.   Thirty-eight-mile transect of vegetational zones from the Rio Grande Valley to the Sangre de Cristo Mountains.

LEGEND

Alpine Tundra

Spruce-fir Forest

Mixed Conifer Forest

Ponderosa Pine Forest

Pinyon-juniper Woodland

Grassland-juniper Ecotone

Short Grass Prairie

Lake Peak
elevation 12,408'

SANGRE DE CRISTO
MOUNTAINS

Santa Fe River

Arroyo Hondo Pueblo
elevation 7090'

Arroyo
Hondo

Santa Fe River

Cochiti Pueblo
elevation 5200'

Rio Grande

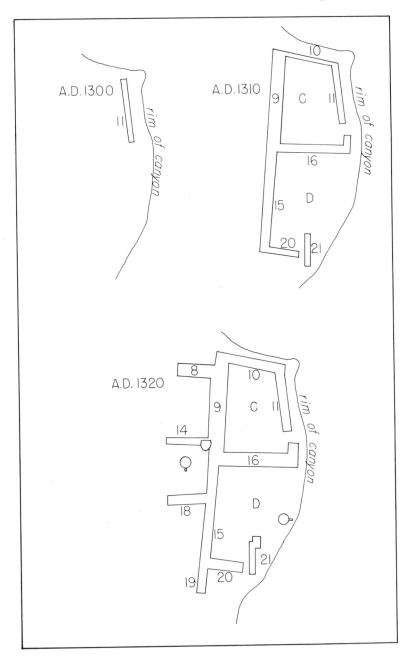

FIG. 3.   Construction sequence at Arroyo Hondo Pueblo, Component I.

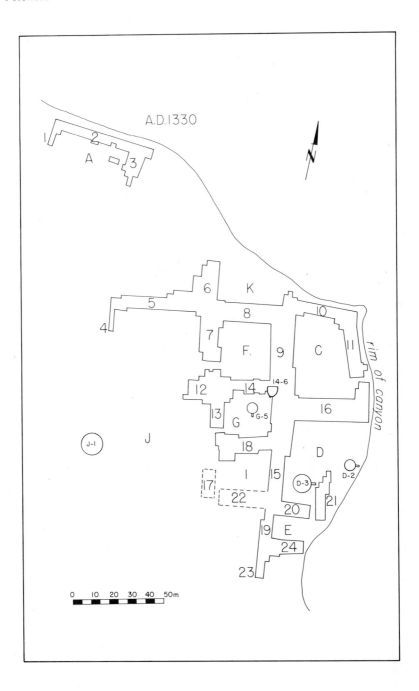

drying and processing, flint knapping, and pottery making. In some plazas and roomblocks were ceremonial kivas, while a larger kivalike structure located about 110 yards west of the pueblo probably served the whole community in a religious capacity.

Clearly, the people prospered at Arroyo Hondo in the early 1300s. Their material remains reflect a well-rounded, largely self-sufficient technology. Potters made a variety of ceramic vessels, mostly culinary, and trade brought both painted and upainted pottery from other pueblos in the region. Stone tools for grinding, cutting, drilling, and scraping were generally made from locally available materials, though obsidian was imported from the Jemez Mountains, 30 miles to the west across the Rio Grande. The bones of game animals and turkeys were made into awls, scrapers, and beads, while small amounts of turquoise for jewelry came from a mine in the hills 15 miles south of Arroyo Hondo. More distant trade connections are evidenced by the presence of scarlet macaws from southern Mexico and abalone and olivella shells from the Pacific Coast and the Gulf of California.

Prosperity at Arroyo Hondo, however, was short-lived. Soon after 1335, as annual precipitation decreased, the town's population began to decline even more dramatically than it had risen. The more recently built roomblocks were abandoned first, and the occupation contracted in the reverse order of the construction sequence. Roofs were dismantled either to reuse the beams or to save steps in obtaining firewood, a task that was becoming increasingly time-consuming because the surrounding woodland had been so extensively cleared. Many deserted rooms were used as refuse dumps, and ceramics from these trash deposits suggest that by 1345, the pueblo was virtually abandoned. For the next 30 years, the ruined pueblo was at most inhabited by a small remnant population, perhaps seasonally, and at times the town may have been vacant. This abandonment marks the end of what we refer to for analytical purposes as the Component I occupation of Arroyo Hondo.

Sometime during the 1370s, another phase of settlement began, termed Component II. Again correlating with a period of increased moisture, this second town was built atop the ruins of the first. By the early 1400s, Arroyo Hondo was once more on its way to becoming an active population center with extensive trade contacts, having grown to two hundred rooms organized in nine roomblocks around three plazas (Fig. 21). But the renewed growth did not continue, for soon after 1410 the region was again affected by drought. As before, rooms were abandoned and demolished as population declined. In about 1420, a catastrophic fire destroyed a large part of the village, and a few years later, the drought reached a severity unprecedented in the history of the pueblo. With this last insult, the second and final occupation of Arroyo Hondo Pueblo came to an end.

THE ARROYO HONDO PROJECT

Research at Arroyo Hondo Pueblo, initiated in 1970, was designed to accomplish four main, interrelated objectives:

1. provide ecological, regional, and chronological perspectives from which to understand the pueblo's sequence of change;
2. develop a detailed base of information about Pueblo culture in the northern Rio Grande region during the pivotal fourteenth-century period of large-settlement growth;
3. examine the causes and effects of the growth, change, and eventual decline of the pueblo;
4. use Arroyo Hondo Pueblo as a case study that could be combined with other archaeological, ethnographic, and historic data to examine the interplay of changes in population, resources, and culture in prehistoric agricultural communities.

The National Science Foundation supported excavation and laboratory work between 1971 and 1974 (grants GC-28001 and GC-42181), and interim results were published in three preliminary reports (Schwartz 1971, 1972; Schwartz and Lang 1973). At the completion of field work, a film entitled *The Rio Grande's Pueblo Past* was made in collaboration with the National Geographic Society, illustrating the history of the project and presenting some initial conclusions. A subsequent National Science Foundation grant (BNS76-83510) provided support for the development and publication of the project results.

To document the project fully, a publication series of 12 volumes was planned, 11 of them to present data and ideas on specific topics and the twelfth to synthesize the results and consider their broader implications. Although each of the first 11 volumes focuses on a particular set of data, it is designed to stand independently as a contribution to northern Rio Grande archaeology. The final book in the series will place Arroyo Hondo Pueblo in historical perspective within the northern Rio Grande, integrate the contributions of the data volumes in terms of the culture and dynamics of the settlement, examine the interrelationships between population growth, resource use, and cultural change at Arroyo Hondo, and consider the cross-cultural implications of rapid growth in agricultural communities. The topics and authors of the Arroyo Hondo volumes are listed as follows.

Contemporary ecology, by N. Edmund Kelley
Site survey, by D. Bruce Dickson, Jr.
Skeletal and mortuary remains, by Ann M. Palkovich
Dendroclimatology, by Martin R. Rose, Jeffrey S. Dean, and William J. Robinson
Faunal analysis, by Richard W. Lang and Arthur H. Harris
Palynology, by Vorsila L. Bohrer
Paleoethnobotany and nutrition, by Wilma E. Wetterstrom
Bone, shell and miscellaneous artifacts, by Christopher S. Causey and Tamsin Venn
Architecture, by John D. Beal
Lithic artifacts, by Laurance D. Linford
Ceramics, by Richard W. Lang
Synthesis, by Douglas W. Schwartz

SKELETAL AND MORTUARY REMAINS

One hundred and twenty human skeletons were excavated at Arroyo Hondo Pueblo, many accompanied by grave goods such as hide blankets, jewelry, and offerings of food. Ann Palkovich's monograph thoroughly describes, analyzes, and interprets these skeletal and mortuary remains. Her analysis led in several interesting directions. An examination of pathologies in relation to the age distribution of the population produced considerations of the impact of malnutrition on the pueblo's demographic structure. Palkovich also used mortuary practices to test an ethnographic model of age and status grading derived from Tewa Pueblo culture, the results providing important insights into the social organization of Arroyo Hondo Pueblo. Finally, the Arroyo Hondo mortuary data were compared with information from other, contemporaneous pueblos in the northern Rio Grande region to examine the existence of a regional pattern.

A similar objective is approached from another direction by James Mackey, who in Appendix G compares the Arroyo Hondo skeletal population with other prehistoric southwestern series. Using a multivariate analysis of 20 discrete, nonmetric cranial traits, Mackey arrives at a measurement of biological distance. His conclusions are consistent with other studies supporting the position that the Arroyo Hondo population was most closely related genetically to Tewa-Tano groups indigenous to the area.

Ann Palkovich has written not just an excellent account of the skeletal and mortuary remains of Arroyo Hondo Pueblo but also a report that goes far beyond mere description to put flesh on the bones of her subjects. One reviewer of an early draft of the manuscript commented that by placing the skeletons "back into their living contexts," Palkovich had impressively combined the "all-too-often estranged perspectives of ethnology, biological anthropology and archaeology into a complete framework of analysis." In doing so, Palkovich has made an important contribution to Rio Grande archaeology and to the study of the physical anthropology of southwestern Indians.

References

DICKSON, D. BRUCE, JR.
1980   *Prehistoric Pueblo Settlement Patterns: The Arroyo Hondo, New Mexico, Site Survey*, Arroyo Hondo Archaeological Series, vol. 2 (Santa Fe: School of American Research Press).

KARLSTROM, THOR N. V., AND JEFFREY S. DEAN
1979   "The Colorado Plateau's Cultural Dynamics and Paleoenvironment," in Euler et al., *Science* 25:1,094 (Fig. 5).

KELLEY, N. EDMUND
1980   *The Contemporary Ecology of Arroyo Hondo, New Mexico*, Arroyo Hondo Archaeological Series, vol. 1 (Santa Fe: School of American Research Press).

SCHWARTZ, DOUGLAS W.
1971   *Background Report on the Archaeology of the Site at Arroyo Hondo: First Arroyo Hondo Field Report* (Santa Fe: School of American Research).

1972   *Archaeological Investigations at the Arroyo Hondo Site: Second Field Report—1971* (Santa Fe: School of American Research).

SCHWARTZ, DOUGLAS W., AND RICHARD W. LANG
1973   *Archaeological Investigations at the Arroyo Hondo Site: Third Field Report—1972* (Santa Fe: School of American Research).

Contents

MAPS AND FIGURES

Contents

Figures

TABLES

Contents

Acknowledgments

It is always a pleasure to see a project come to fruition. My association with the Arroyo Hondo project has been a valuable, rewarding, and very enjoyable experience. First, I am sincerely grateful to Dr. Douglas W. Schwartz for asking me to participate in this project. His unflagging interest in and support of my research made the completion and publication of this work possible. The staff of the Arroyo Hondo Project and the School of American Research have become good friends and colleagues; they made my summers in Santa Fe a truly enjoyable experience. I would like to thank them all for their help, advice, and friendship.

Earlier drafts of this monograph were reviewed by John Beal, the late Wanda Driskell, William Howells, Jane Kepp, Richard Lang, Erik Reed, Douglas Schwartz, Philip Shultz, James Spuhler, and Eric DeVor. The considerable time and energy they spent commenting on my work has been a great help to me in revising this monograph. This volume is a tribute to their efforts, interest in this research, and patience. I extend to all of them my sincere thanks. A grateful word of thanks to Jane Kepp, Phillip Brittenham, and the late Wanda Driskell. Their editing of this volume tranformed my own peculiar writing style into respectable English. The excellent photography was done by David Noble. Richard Lang demonstrated one of his talents by doing the fine line drawings. Map 2 and Figures 1 and 3 were drawn by Rachel

Conine, and Dan Palkovich drew Figure 15. My sincere thanks to them for their careful, thoughtful work. A special thanks to my parents for all their support and understanding. As always, any remaining errors and shortcomings of this work are solely my responsibility.

The Arroyo Hondo Project was supported by NSF grants GC-28001 and GC-42181. Publication of the Arroyo Hondo monograph series was made possible by NSF grant BNS76-82510. Additional research by the writer was supported, in part, by a Smithsonian Pre-doctoral Fellowship in Anthropology.

1

Introduction

Between 1970 and 1974, the School of American Research carried out an archaeological project and related multidisciplinary studies at Arroyo Hondo Pueblo, the site of a large fourteenth-century community. Among the materials recovered during the four years of excavation were 120 burials and over two hundred isolated human bones scattered throughout the site. This monograph presents the skeletal and mortuary data recorded upon excavation and later osteological analysis and examines the data for information about population dynamics and social structure at Arroyo Hondo Pueblo.

Occupied between A.D. 1300 and 1425, the pueblo spanned the later part of what Wendorf and Reed (1955) termed the Coalition Period (A.D. 1200–1325) and the early part of the Classic Period (A.D. 1325–1600). During its history, the town was first inhabited by a large group of people between about A.D. 1300 and 1350, was then either severely depopulated or completely abandoned, and finally was occupied by a smaller group between about A.D. 1370 and 1425. The period between A.D. 1300 and 1370 is referred to as Component I, the remainder of the occupation as Component II.

Of the 120 burials excavated at Arroyo Hondo, 108 were associated with Component I, and 12 were associated with Component II. All individuals were found in formal graves, with the exception of nine who appeared to have been the victims of accidents. Flexed or semi-

1

flexed inhumation was almost universal. Beyond these generalizations, no single burial pattern can be described as typical. Of the formal interments that were recovered, nearly half were in plaza areas, and the remainder occurred about equally in subfloor pits in rooms and trash deposits in either rooms or plazas. The bodies were more commonly placed with head to the east (37 percent of those for which orientation could be determined), but all the cardinal directions were well represented. Seventy of the individuals (63 percent) had been buried with grave accoutrements, of which hide blankets and yucca-fiber mats were the commonest.

In terms of age and sex distribution, 67 of the individuals were subadults, defined as those under 15 years of age (that is, pre-reproductive), and 53 were adults. Among the adults for whom sex could be determined, 27 were females, 18 males. Infant mortality appeared to be quite high; also high was the incidence of skeletal pathologies, which were observed in almost 47 percent of the 120 burials.

OBJECTIVES OF THE STUDY

A primary objective of this study is to present a thorough description of the Arroyo Hondo skeletal and mortuary remains (chapter 2). As one of the few well-documented collections in the Southwest in which all excavated materials have been retained for study, the Arroyo Hondo skeletal series is a valuable research resource. This report is intended to make the data available to those studying various aspects of population dynamics, the spatial patterning of Pueblo interments, or other bio-cultural aspects of prehistoric Pueblo society.

The analytical focus of the study involves certain biocultural characteristics of the largest portion of the skeletal sample, the 108 individuals associated with Component I. First, the skeletal remains were examined for evidence of dietary stress, which was then related to the demographic structure and disease patterns of the Arroyo Hondo population. Clinical and ethnographic studies suggest that certain skeletal pathologies and bone reactions reflect nutritional deficiencies and may be interpreted as evidence of malnutrition in prehistoric populations. Nutrition-related pathologies were particularly common among the subadults buried at Arroyo Hondo Pueblo. This observation leads to the suggestion that malnutrition was a major cause of the high infant and child mortality seen in life tables constructed for the pueblo's population (chapter 3).

Second, it was hypothesized that in its social organization, Arroyo Hondo exhibited a set of age and status grades similar to those of historic eastern Pueblo groups, as described by Ortiz (1969). Statistical tests of the mortuary data and other observations tended to support this hypothesis, suggesting that some degree of age and ceremonial-status stratification was practiced at the pueblo (chapter 4). If Arroyo Hondo can be considered typical of the large, northern Rio Grande towns of the fourteenth century, then the results of both this analysis and the demographic study probably apply to the region as a whole during the late Coalition and early Classic periods.

In an effort to determine whether the skeletal and mortuary material from Arroyo Hondo was indeed representative of the region, the literature on some nearby pueblos contemporaneous with Arroyo Hondo was briefly reviewed. Although factors such as varying completeness of reporting, different excavation strategies, and differential preservation prevented systematic comparison, it appears that Arroyo Hondo fits the general pattern of mortuary practices in the fourteenth-century northern Rio Grande area. A possible exception to this generalization may be a greater incidence of grave accoutrements at Arroyo Hondo than elsewhere. The concluding chapter of this volume (chapter 5) presents the comparative data that place Arroyo Hondo Pueblo in its regional context.

THE EXCAVATION OF BURIALS AT ARROYO HONDO PUEBLO

In 1915, Nels C. Nelson, of the American Museum of Natural History, conducted the first documented excavations at Arroyo Hondo Pueblo. His field notes state that "over 30 skeletons, representing all ages were exhumed" (Nelson 1915:5), but he recorded specific information for only 12 individuals. In addition, he noted "traces of skeletons" along the northeast corner of the site, apparently washing out of the trash middens on the steep slopes of the arroyo.

Most of Nelson's work concentrated on rooms. The sketchy information in his field notes indicates that he excavated 101 rooms dating to the first occupation of the site and 12 representing the second

3

occupation. All 12 burials discussed by Nelson in his notes apparently dated to the first occupation. Of these burials, four were located in the trash fill of rooms, two were found in midden areas, and five seem to have been the victims of room collapses in roomblocks 16 and 19. Only one individual can be designated a subfloor interment.

It is somewhat surprising that Nelson noted only 30 burials in all his excavations at Arroyo Hondo. It must be kept in mind, however, that the major objective of his work was to establish a prehistoric pottery chronology for this part of the Southwest. He conducted room excavations to obtain large pottery samples, and it is uncertain whether all potential burial locations, such as subfloor pits, were thoroughly investigated.

Following the standard practice of his time, Nelson recorded little information on the burials and their contexts. None of the burials were assigned catalog numbers. Although one skeleton was noted as having been "kept," most of the remains were apparently reburied. A few of these bones were found in some of Nelson's backfilled rooms that were reexcavated by the School of American Research. Because of the lack of the skeletal material and the absence of detailed records, little information from Nelson's work could be incorporated into this study. Appendix A presents the data that are available from his notes.

The School of American Research excavations at Arroyo Hondo Pueblo, conducted between 1970 and 1974, covered a wide range of functional and spatial proveniences. Rooms, traditionally the focus of pueblo excavations, provide an important but only partial view of the culture of a community. The goals of the Arroyo Hondo project demanded a broader excavation strategy that included plazas and trash middens in addition to rooms. The sampling design called for the excavation of at least one room in each roomblock and groups of contiguous rooms in five locations. A series of maps showing overall site configuration and areas excavated is presented in Appendix B. A large part of the Component I plaza G was cleared, as were smaller areas in plazas A, D, and K and the Component II plaza C. Trash deposits inside and outside of the plazas were also tested.

This excavation strategy made possible the recovery of a fairly large collection of burials from varied proveniences over the entire site. Plazas and some trash deposits proved to be especially productive for a mortuary study. Because formal, discrete cemeteries are seldom found in prehistoric Pueblo sites, sampling of widespread proveniences allows the distribution and patterning of burials to be examined. Occasionally clusters of interments are found, but these seem to reflect the suitability of a location for burials, such as a corner of a plaza, rather than the selection of that area as a formal cemetery.

The recovery of burials at Arroyo Hondo Pueblo was an objective in its own right, not merely as a by-product of excavation for other purposes. Although areas to be sampled were not chosen strictly for their potential to produce burials, that potential was often one factor among several that influenced the choice. During the 1973 and 1974 field seasons, the author personally conducted or supervised the excavation of all human skeletal remains. When a burial was located, all soil within the burial pit or surrounding the skeleton, if no pit could be delimited, was screened. Information on body orientation, burial context, grave accoutrements, and so forth was systematically recorded for each interment (see Appendix D). The state of skeletal preservation, which varied throughout the site, was also noted for each individual. All skeletal remains and associated artifacts were retained for further analysis.

Each skeleton or isolated bone was assigned an identification number such as 12-G-2-4-12 or 12-16-38-6. In each case, the first entry indicates the site, LA 12, and the second entry the plaza (letter designation) or roomblock (number designation) in which the individual was found. The third number in roomblock designations is the number of the room itself. In plaza identifications, the third entry indicates either a particular feature, such as kiva 12-G-5, or an excavated grid square. Thus, the preceding examples refer to burials found in plaza G, feature 2 (the gateway area), and in roomblock 16, room 38. Any subsequent numbers or letters carry a variety of information that is too complex to be explained here; these portions of the specimen numbers are best considered simply as identification per se.

In summary, this monograph: (1) provides comprehensive data on the skeletal remains and associated mortuary practices found during the School of American Research excavations at Arroyo Hondo Pueblo, (2) presents analyses focusing on problems of health and social organization in this prehistoric pueblo, and (3) characterizes Arroyo Hondo in its larger social context of fourteenth-century Pueblo occupation in the northern Rio Grande region. The volume provides a context for further research into the nature of Pueblo population and society.

FIG. 4. Young adult male (12-D-1-7) buried in trash deposit in plaza.

2

The Arroyo Hondo Skeletal and Mortuary Remains

A total of 120 burials was recovered from Arroyo Hondo Pueblo during the School of American Research excavations. Of these, 108 burials were associated with the earlier occupation of the site (Component I), including 99 individuals recovered from formal graves and 9 found covered with rubble, apparently representing accidental deaths. Twelve individuals were found in formal graves dating to the reoccupation of Arroyo Hondo (Component II). More than two hundred isolated human bones supplemented the burial sample. A few burials appeared to have been disinterred or disturbed by the pueblo's prehistoric inhabitants.

All formal burials were primary, single-individual interments (Fig. 4). They were typically found in oval-shaped pits with flat bottoms and straight sides. Pit outlines in homogenous trash deposits could not be defined but were likely oval as well. With few exceptions, burial pits were just large enough to accommodate the flexed body of the individual (see Appendix D for measurements). Pits containing subadults were smaller than those containing adult burials because the flexed body position was uniformly maintained regardless of the age or size of the individual. Body position (right side, left side, and so forth) and orientation (cardinal direction of the head) varied throughout the site. To some extent, subadults typically lay on the right side, adults on the left side. Approximately one-third of all burials were oriented to the east. Preservation of both skeletal remains and organic grave accoutrements such as animal hide and plant materials also varied among the burials. Because of differing skeletal preservation, the criteria used to assess age and sex necessarily varied between individuals, depending on the skeletal parts recovered.

The following sections present information by occupational component on the locations of burials, body position and orientation, grave accoutrements, accidental deaths, age, sex, pathologies, and isolated remains.

LOCATIONS OF BURIALS

Three general kinds of proveniences contained skeletal remains: plazas, rooms, and trash middens. Table 1 gives the numbers of adults and subadults found in each type of location in each component. In Appendix B, figures 16 through 21 show the exact locations of burials by component, keyed to a list of individual specimen numbers.

Component I Plazas

Three of the nine plaza areas associated with the first and largest occupation of the site were excavated, plazas A and K partially and plaza G almost entirely. Plaza A, associated with roomblocks 1, 2, and

TABLE 1.
Locations of formal burials at Arroyo Hondo Pueblo.

	Plazas	Rooms	Trash Middens	Trash-Filled Rooms
COMPONENT I				
Subadults	33	18	8	3
Adults	15	5	15	2
Total	48	23	23	5
COMPONENT II				
Subadults	3	1	2	0
Adults	5	0	1	0
Total	8	1	3	0
Total, All Burials	56	24	26	5

3, lies to the northwest of the main portion of the site and was used from approximately the A.D. 1320s through the 1330s. About 16 cubic meters of fill were removed in the northeast corner of the plaza. No interments were recovered, although excavation by Nels Nelson in roomblocks 1, 2, and 3 had yielded three burials.

Plaza K is located at the northern edge of the site, bordered by roomblocks 6, 8, and a small portion of 9. It is open to the north and appears to have extended to the rim of the Arroyo Hondo. Plaza K was first used at about A.D. 1320 and was abandoned between 1330 and 1350. A total of 44 cubic meters of fill was excavated along the south and west walls of the plaza, and three major plaza surfaces were found superimposed. The earliest surface represents the initial use of the plaza mainly as a source of adobe for room construction. The second surface was used primarily for domestic activities, and the latest, uppermost surface contained evidence mainly of the remains of turkey pens. Trash deposits and adobe wash covered the entire area.

Ten burials were found in plaza K, nine of them subadults and one adult. All were associated with the second (middle) plaza surface and date to about A.D. 1335–1345. They represent the last major activity associated with this surface and in some cases intrude upon earlier features.

Plaza G, the smallest Component I plaza, had a depositional history ranging from about A.D. 1310–15 to sometime in the 1350s. It is enclosed by roomblocks 13, 14, 15A, and 18. Excavation removed approximately 465 cubic meters of fill in plaza G, with most of the work concentrated along the walls of the surrounding roomblocks. The plaza surfaces and postplaza trash deposits contained 38 burials.

Apparently most of plaza G saw activity throughout the first occupation of Arroyo Hondo Pueblo, resulting in a stratigraphic series of use surfaces, zones of compacted soil, and trash lenses. Despite the stratigraphic complexity of the plaza, it was possible during excavation to identify three major, well-preserved use surfaces. All activity areas and plaza features were associated with one of these three primary surface levels. Since it was impossible to discern the order of interment of all the burials in plaza G, they were grouped according to the primary plaza surface with which they were most likely associated.

Because the use surfaces in plaza G were numbered as they were encountered during excavation, the earliest is primary plaza surface 3. It dates between A.D. 1310 and 1315 and overlies the original ground surface, small trash lenses, or, in some places, trash-filled borrow pits. During the use of surface 3, the plaza seems to have functioned as a marginal activity area, exhibiting few plaza features. Some trash filling of borrow pits may have occurred. Also, the construction and use of a subterranean kiva in plaza G (kiva 12-G-5) appears to be associated with or slightly to postdate this major surface. Six subadult burials and one adult were found in pits that had been dug into primary plaza surface 3.

Next in the stratigraphic sequence, primary plaza surface 2 dates from approximately A.D. 1315 to 1330. Greater domestic activity during this time is indicated by an increased number and variety of features such as milling bins. It was possible to associate ten subadult and three adult burials with this surface.

The uppermost surface, primary plaza surface 1, represents the last major use of plaza G. Numerous and diverse plaza features were built on this surface, which is overlain in places with midden deposits. Tree-ring dates place the use of surface 1 from A.D. 1330 to 1348+, with no domestic activities occurring in plaza G after that time. Associated with this surface were six subadult and seven adult interments. Five burials—three subadults and two adults—postdated the use of surface 1, apparently having been interred in the trash deposits overlying it.

In addition to the burials from plazas G and K, three adults and a subadult from plaza C and a subadult associated with plaza D bring the total number of Component I plaza interments to 48. Of these, 33 (68.8 percent) were subadults, and 15 (31.2 percent) were adults. It is important to note that these 48 individuals make up 48.5 percent of the total of 99 formal burials dating to Component I. There seems to have been a strong tendency to inter individuals in plazas close to the walls of rooms. Plaza corners in particular yielded a large number of burials. On the other hand, no burials were found in the vicinities of gates, which were the passageways between roomblocks leading into plazas; and none occurred in the northeast corner of plaza G adjacent to kiva 12-14-6, a D-shaped surface kiva in roomblock 14.

Component I Rooms

Rooms with subfloor interments were other important grave locations at Arroyo Hondo, yielding 23.2 percent of all formal Component I burials. Fifty-nine Component I rooms, containing 368 square me-

10

ters of floor area, were excavated, and 14 of the rooms yielded 23 individuals. Five rooms produced more than one burial (Fig. 5). Twenty of the individuals were formal subfloor interments, including 15 subadults and 5 adults. In nearly all cases, association between the burial and the room was clear, a pit having been dug through the floor into the ground below (Fig. 6). In just six cases were the pits found plastered over, and only these rooms seem to have been reused after the interment. Furthermore, only the reused rooms dated prior to A.D. 1330. No other burial pits showed evidence of having been plastered, suggesting that the rooms containing them were abandoned after the burial, probably during the later part of Component I or about A.D. 1330–1350. The remaining three individuals were recovered from the fallen second-story roof of a room in roomblock 6. All three were preterm fetuses that had apparently been aborted and buried in the soil covering the roof.

FIG. 5. Burial 12-16-36-4-1. Adult male in subfloor pit, body painted before interment. On left is unusual pit containing part of a disturbed burial (12-16-36-5-2).

11

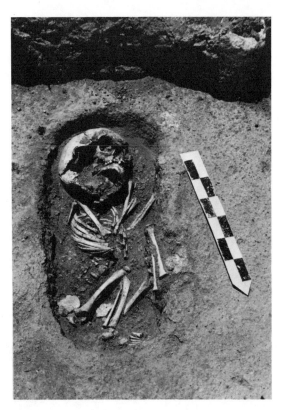

FIG. 6. Young child
(12-21-3-III-1) buried in
subfloor pit.

Component I Trash Deposits

Twenty-eight individuals—11 subadults (39.3 percent) and 17 adults
(60.7 percent)—were found in Component I trash deposits at Arroyo
Hondo Pueblo. Borrow pits left from quarrying adobe for room construction were commonly employed as refuse dumps, as were depres-
sions formed by collapsed kivas and, at times, abandoned rooms or
roomblocks. Badly eroded midden areas along the steep sides of the
arroyo bordering the site were also observed. Burials were recovered
from all such locations, from which a total of 127 cubic meters of fill
was removed in various parts of the site. Unfortunately, burial pits
were seldom observed in trash middens, making it difficult to associate
the burials with specific, dated episodes of deposition. However, all
the midden interments belonged to the Component I occupation of
Arroyo Hondo, as indicated by pottery types found in the trash surrounding the burials.

Component II Plazas

Plaza C was the scene of activity during both components I and II, its later use falling between about A.D. 1370 and the 1420s. It is the only Component II plaza completely delimited by roomblocks and the only one extensively excavated at Arroyo Hondo. About 45 cubic meters of fill were removed along the north, east, and west walls of plaza C. Eight of the 12 Component II burials (66.7 percent) came from various use surfaces in this plaza.

Four major surfaces dating to the second occupation were identified. The major activity associated with surface 1, the earliest or lowermost, was the use of turkey pens between about A.D. 1374 and 1387. Some trash filling of borrow pits toward the center of the plaza may also have taken place at this time. Four adult burials were found in this plaza surface.

Plaza surface 2, dating to A.D. 1387 or slightly later, exhibited many diverse features reflecting mainly domestic activities. This surface contained the burial pits of three subadults. Above it was surface 3, on which evidence of turkey pens again appeared but which had no associated burials. Finally, plaza surface 4, dating after A.D. 1415, yielded evidence of very limited domestic activity at a time when either the site was intermittently occupied or this area of plaza C was used only occasionally. One adult burial was associated with surface 4.

It appears that the inhabitants of Arroyo Hondo Pueblo after A.D. 1370, like their earlier counterparts, tended to bury their dead in pits along the walls bordering plazas. Fewer interments are found as one moves toward the center of plaza C, and only burials in the trash fill of borrow pits occur any distance from the walls of roomblocks.

Component II Rooms

Forty-one Component II rooms, or 269 square meters of floor area, were excavated at Arroyo Hondo. These figures represent 69.5 percent of all Component II rooms and 73.3 percent of their total floor space, yet only one burial, a child in roomblock 10, was found in a subfloor pit. This scarcity of subfloor burials in rooms suggests that mortuary customs during the second occupation of the pueblo were in some respects distinctly different from those seen earlier.

Component II Trash Deposits

Few midden areas were associated with the Component II occupation, the major ones being those in borrow pits in plaza C. In these trash-filled pits were found two subadult burials (Fig. 7) and one adult burial, making up 25 percent of all Component II individuals. It is possible that other trash deposits lying closer to the site surface had eroded away. This suggestion is supported by the tendency for Component II rooms to be found in much more deteriorated condition than the deeper, sometimes underlying Component I structures. Differential preservation might to some extent account for the apparent absence of other categories of skeletal remains, such as accidental deaths and roof burials, in Component II deposits.

FIG. 7. Infant (12-C-A-6-1-1) buried in trash-filled borrow pit in plaza, Component II.

14

TABLE 2.
Body positions of Arroyo Hondo burials.

	Left Side		Right Side		On Face		On Back		Unknown		Total
COMPONENT I											
Subadults	12	(19%)	20	(32%)	5	(8%)	7	(11%)	18	(29%)	62
Adults	9	(24%)	5	(13%)	4	(11%)	8	(22%)	11	(30%)	37
Total	21	(21%)	25	(25%)	9	(9%)	15	(15%)	29	(29%)	99
COMPONENT II											
Subadults	2		2		0		2		0		6
Adults	2		0		4		0		0		6
Total	4		2		4		2		0		12
Total	25	(23%)	27	(24%)	13	(12%)	17	(15%)	29	(26%)	111

BODY POSITION AND ORIENTATION

Tables 2 and 3 summarize the body positions and head orientation to a cardinal direction for the Arroyo Hondo burials. Of the individuals for whom body position could be determined, Component I subadults most often lay on the right side, head to the east. Adults during this occupation were often placed on the left side or the back with head to the east. One individual in plaza K was buried in an extended position (Fig. 8), but the discernible position of all other Component I interments was flexed or semiflexed.

With so few individuals dating to Component II, it is difficult to point out tendencies in position with any reliability. However, east appears to be the predominant head direction, and all bodies were flexed. It seems unusual that so many Component II adults were placed facedown for burial.

TABLE 3.
Head orientation of Arroyo Hondo burials.

	North		South		East		West		Unknown		Total
COMPONENT I											
Subadults	14	(23%)	9	(14%)	22	(36%)	8	(13%)	9	(14%)	62
Adults	2	(5%)	7	(19%)	12	(32%)	5	(14%)	11	(30%)	37
Total	16	(16%)	16	(16%)	34	(34%)	13	(13%)	20	(20%)	99
COMPONENT II											
Subadults	0		2		3		1		0		6
Adults	1		1		4		0		0		6
Total	1		3		7		1		0		12
Total	17	(15%)	19	(17%)	41	(37%)	14	(13%)	20	(18%)	111

FIG. 8. Young adult male (12-K-16-V-1) buried beneath plaza surface, the only extended burial in the collection.

GRAVE ACCOUTREMENTS

Seventy individuals at Arroyo Hondo Pueblo were found buried with grave accoutrements of various kinds (Figs. 9 and 10). Of the 99 Component I burials, 63 contained grave goods: 45 of the 61 subadults and 18 of the 38 adults. Seven of the twelve Component II individuals, including five of the six subadults and two of six adults, had mortuary items.

The artifact assemblage accompanying the burials was not particularly impressive, as is true of assemblages recovered from other sites of this time period in the northern Rio Grande region. Animal-hide blankets and yucca-fiber mats (Figs. 11 and 12) were prevalent, especially among the subadults (Table 4). Mats and blankets could clearly be seen to cover or encase the entire body rather than being fitted around portions of the body, as would be the case for clothing. Pottery sherds, usually decorated wares, occurred with 13 individuals, and

16

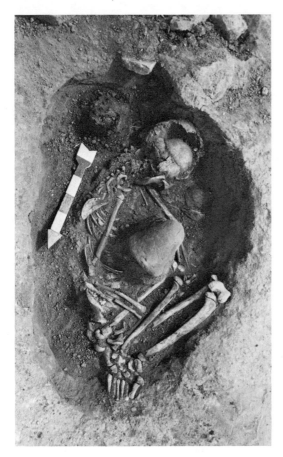

FIG. 9. Child (12-G-2-3-27) buried in trash deposit in plaza with "fire-dog" or clay pot support.

plant remains, probably representing food offerings, were found with 10. Shell ornaments appeared exclusively with subadults, but stone beads and pendants were found with both age groups. Two adults exhibited traces of paint that had been applied to the bodies before burial.

The most elaborate set of artifacts accompanied a Component I adult male. The 16 items included projectile points, the possible remains of a wood bow, stone balls and sheets of mica, a bone awl tip, an eagle claw, the skin of a raven, and the wings of a second raven. Such an assemblage suggests that this individual had some special ceremonial status in life.

FIG. 10. Adult female (12-18-8-VI-1) buried in subfloor pit with "firedog" or clay pot support.

ACCIDENTAL DEATHS

Two groups of skeletal remains were uncovered that did not fit the expected range of formal mortuary practices. In roomblock 16, two adults found on the floor of a room in the northernmost row, adjacent to plaza C, had apparently been killed when the room collapsed (Fig. 13). In the next room to the east, Nelson had recovered the remains of two adults and two subadults. The positions of the bodies suggested that all these individuals may have been asleep at the time of the collapse. Wall and roof rubble lay directly over the remains. Sometime later, the area was leveled and another series of rooms built on top of the fallen ones.

The remains of at least five individuals and isolated remains possibly

FIG. 11.   Matting adhering to side of burial pit.

FIG. 12. Detail of matting from another burial. Fragment on left is approximately 20 cm long.

TABLE 4.

Number of individuals accompanied by each type of grave accoutre-
ment. (Some graves contained more than one type of item.)

| Item | COMPONENT I | | COMPONENT II | | Total |
	Subadults	Adults	Subadults	Adults	
Hide blanket	24	5	0	0	29
Yucca-fiber mat	19	6	3	1	29
Pot or potsherd	8	4	0	1	13
Plant remains	7	2	1	0	10
Stone artifacts	2	5	0	0	7
Jet, turquoise	1	2	1	0	4
Shell ornaments	3	0	1	0	4
Wooden objects	2	2	0	0	4
Bone artifacts	1	1	0	0	2
Feathers	2	0	0	0	2
Body paint	0	2	0	0	2
Pipe or cloud blower	0	1	0	0	1
Painted gourd	1	0	0	0	1
Animal remains	0	1	0	0	1
Other material	3	2	1	0	6

representing two additional individuals were found lying on or just
above the floor of kiva 12-G-5 (Fig. 14). Stone slabs and small amounts
of wall rubble and roof material covered some of the bodies. The cause
of these individuals' deaths clearly was sudden trauma. They may have
been inside the already abandoned, dilapidated kiva, perhaps recover-
ing wood or ceremonial items, when the remaining walls and roof
collapsed on them. Such an accident would account both for the
stones and rubble found on the skeletons and for the fact that large
quantities of wall and roof rubble were not noted during excavation. It
is also possible that sometime after the collapse of the kiva, the area
was partially cleared and perhaps some bodies removed. This would
account for the articulated portions of skeletons that were found. The
individuals discovered during excavation were simply those not removed by the prehistoric inhabitants. Eventually the depression left by
the kiva was filled with trash, and the remains of some burials and
isolated bones were recovered from higher levels in this midden deposit.

Another possibility is that the individuals in kiva 12-G-5 were the
victims of some kind of internal or external group strife. The stone
slabs might have been thrown on them as they stood in the open pit of
the kiva. However, one would expect to find formal weapons such as
projectile points or the stone heads of clubs also associated with vio-

FIG. 13.   Two adult females killed in collapse of room 12-16-37.

lence of this sort. At other prehistoric southwestern pueblos, victims of social strife were often trapped in buildings and burned to death. At Arroyo Hondo, neither weapons nor evidence of burning of the kiva was noted. Furthermore, there was no skeletal evidence such as broken bones or embedded projectile points indicating violence. Death due to warfare, therefore, seems unlikely.

SKELETAL INFORMATION

A number of standard skeletal observations were made for the Arroyo Hondo collection: the age and sex of each individual, gross pathologies, and some skeletal metrics. The age and sex criteria, measuring procedures, and stature estimation standards used in this study are outlined in Appendix C, which also presents the long-bone measurements (maximum length) collected for stature estimates. Cranial metrics were collected for a study by James Mackey (see Appendix G) and are also listed in Appendix C. The extremely small sample of whole,

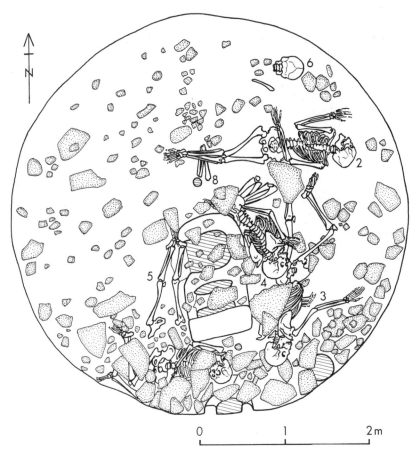

FIG. 14. Distribution of skeletal remains on floor of kiva 12-G-5. Rocks are stippled, other features hatched.

measurable crania, along with the skewing of measurements that is introduced by artificial cranial deformation during infancy, did not warrant a detailed metric study of the Arroyo Hondo crania beyond Mackey's work. To check for accuracy, the writer aged and sexed the entire collection three times independently.

Observations on selected skeletal pathologies are included for each individual in Appendix D and are summarized in Appendix F. Since a major analytical focus of this study involved population stress, pathologies associated with dietary and disease stress were emphasized. Other skeletal pathologies, specifically osteoarthritis and dental disease, were present in the Arroyo Hondo population but were not recorded for this study. Selected skeletal anomalies were noted and are included in the skeletal information for each individual (Appendix D).

Component I

Nearly half the Component I mortuary population—49 out of 108 individuals— consisted of individuals who died before the age of five (Table 5). This is a rather high infant-child mortality rate, but apparently it is not particularly unusual for a prehistoric or preindustrial population (Krzywicki 1934). Of the 40 Component I adults for whom sex could be ascertained, 24 were female and 16 were male. To test the sample for imbalance in the male-female sex ratio, a chi-square test suggested by Lovejoy (1971) was used. This test assumes a one-to-one ratio of the sexes for adults, which is biologically acceptable.

When only the individuals derived from formal burials were tested, the difference between the observed and expected numbers of males and females in the mortuary population was not statistically significant (Table 6). Adding in the individuals who had met with accidental

TABLE 5.
The age and sex distribution of individuals associated with each component.

| Age | COMPONENT I | | | | COMPONENT II | | | |
	M	F	Unknown	Total	M	F	Unknown	Total
0–1	—	—	—	29	—	—	—	2
1–4.9	—	—	—	20	—	—	—	3
5–9.9	—	—	—	5	—	—	—	1
10–14.9	—	—	—	7	—	—	—	0
15–19.9	3	0	1	4	0	0	1	1
20–24.9	1	1	1	3	2	0	0	2
25–29.9	1	2	0	3	0	0	0	0
30–34.9	3	1	0	4	0	0	0	0
35–39.9	2	8	0	10	0	0	0	0
40–44.9	1	1	0	2	0	1	0	1
45–49.9	1	3	0	4	0	1	0	1
50+	0	2	0	2	0	1	0	1
Adult, age unknown	4	6	5	15	0	0	0	0
Total	16	24	7	108	2	3	1	12

TABLE 6.
Chi-square test of observed versus expected sex distribution of adults from formal mortuary contexts only, Component I.

	Male	Female	Total
Observed	14	17	31
Expected	15.5	15.5	31
Difference	1.5	1.5	

$\chi^2 = 0.2903$
Significance level approximately 0.60

death gave a higher but still statistically insignificant chi-square value (Table 7). Both tests indicated that there was no statistically significant skewing of the adult sex ratio at Arroyo Hondo Pueblo.

The stature of the Component I adult population ranged between 145 cm and 170 cm, with an average of 159 cm (62.6 in.). For males, the range was 156.78 cm to 171.92 cm, the average 163.87 cm (64.5 in.). Female height ranged from 148.68 cm to 162.25 cm, with a mean of 156.24 cm (61.5 in.). Stature estimates were made only for those individuals who did not manifest any major skeletal alteration due to either pathology or postmortem breakage. Consequently, individuals with pathological bowing of the limbs were excluded from the stature estimates. The standard for stature reconstruction is based on a study of indigenous Indian populations from Mexico (Genovés 1967; see also Appendix C). This standard has been employed in studies of other prehistoric southwestern skeletal series (Bennett 1973b) and is the best one available for such populations.

Pathologies of various kinds appeared in 49 Component I individuals (44 percent), including 31 subadults and 17 adults. Six of the pathologies listed in Table 8 are associated with nutritional or disease

TABLE 7.
Chi-square test of observed versus expected sex distribution of all adults, Component I.

	Male	Female	Total
Observed	16	24	40
Expected	20	20	40
Difference	4	4	

$\chi^2 = 1.60$
Significance level approximately 0.20

TABLE 8.

Number of individuals exhibiting each type of skeletal pathology. (Some individuals exhibit more than one pathology.)

| | COMPONENT I | | COMPONENT II | | |
	Subadult	Adult	Subadult	Adult	Total
Bowing of the Long Bones	5	9	0	1	15
Porotic Hyperostosis	10	0	4	0	14
Porosity	13	0	0	0	13
Endocranial Lesion	8	0	1	0	9
Cribra Orbitalia	6	1	2	0	9
Localized Periostitis	2	2	1	0	5
Widespread Periostitis	3	0	0	0	3
Osteoma	0	2	0	1	3
Localized Resorptive Lesion	0	2	0	0	2
Local Osteomyelitis	0	2	0	0	2
Osteochondroma	0	1	0	0	1
Auditory Exostoses	1	0	0	0	1
Dislocation	0	1	0	0	1
Embedded Projectile Point	0	1	0	0	1

stresses: bowing of the long bones, porotic hyperostosis, porosity, endocranial lesions, cribra orbitalia, and periostitis. The incidence of pathologies in the subadult and adult age groups indicates a marked difference in the health status of these two segments of the population. Subadults showed nearly equal or greater incidence of each type of pathology than did the adult population of Component I. Greater susceptibility to disease and undernutrition probably created severe health problems in the younger age groups.

Component II

Because only 12 individuals dating to the second occupation at Arroyo Hondo were found, no reliable generalizations about age or sex distribution can be made. Average stature during this period, based on two adult males and two adult females, was 159.55 cm, very close to the average height of Component I adults. The mean male height was 165.64 cm, the female mean 153.47 cm. Again, presumably because of the small skeletal sample, not all pathologies appeared in Component II individuals. Still, the general pattern of pathologies was similar to that of Component I, with more subadults than adults exhibiting pathologies.

ISOLATED REMAINS

Over two hundred isolated human bones and bone fragments were recovered at Arroyo Hondo Pueblo, usually from trash deposits. Occasionally several bones of one individual occurred together, and in one case, some isolated remains overlying an interment later proved to belong to that individual. A count of the isolated remains by body part (Table 9) indicates that among the adult material, small bones such as those of the hands and feet were commonest. However, some large bones, including several crania, were recovered in extraburial contexts. Among the subadult bones, the various body parts were more evenly represented.

On the evidence of the isolated human remains, it appears that disturbance of burials by the occupants of Arroyo Hondo Pueblo was not a particularly rare event. Some disregard for the exhumed remains

TABLE 9.
Isolated human remains.

	COMPONENT I		COMPONENT II	
	Subadult	Adult	Subadult	Adult
Cranium	7	13	2	3
Arm	4	2	1	1
Hand	6	13	0	5
Leg	3	1	4	3
Foot	8	24	1	4
Vertebra	7	16	7	4
Rib	7	5	1	0
Unidentified Long Bone	0	0	0	1
Tooth	3	15	1	6
Mandible	2	3	0	0
Pelvis	3	9	0	0
Sternum	0	1	0	1
Patella	0	2	0	0
Scapula	3	0	0	0
Clavicle	3	0	0	0

NOTE: In addition to the remains listed above, eight clusters of bones were recovered, each representing a single individual. Four of the clusters—two hands and two feet— were adult bones, and four comprising various body parts were subadult. All were associated with Component I.

is evident in the casual disposal of the disturbed bones. Small bones seem most likely to have been incorporated into the trash middens.

SUMMARY AND DISCUSSION

During the first occupation of Arroyo Hondo Pueblo, individuals buried in plazas typically were those under the age of 15, their bodies oriented to the east and usually accompanied by hide blankets, jewelry, food, or other grave goods. Burials beneath the floors of rooms, next commonest after plaza interments, tended to be subadults and adult females, again oriented to the east. Grave goods were often found with these individuals. Two adult males with unusual grave accoutrements were also found in subfloor pits in rooms. Both adults and subadults were buried in trash middens, where they were oriented to no predominant direction and seldom accompanied by mortuary goods.

No similar generalizations can be made for the second occupation of the pueblo because of its unreliably small sample of burials. However, in one respect, Component II mortuary practices seemed to differ considerably from those of Component I. During the earlier occupation, interments were divided between outside locations (plazas and trash middens) and rooms, whereas the exterior locations seemed definitely to have been preferred during the later occupation. The figures in Table 10 show that although much greater plaza areas and volumes of trash were excavated for Component I, the number of Component I burials per unit of fill was only about half that of Component II. Only

TABLE 10.
Comparison of Component I and II burial locations.

Plazas and Trash Deposits		
	COMPONENT I	COMPONENT II
Volume Excavated	651.8 m³	45.0 m³
Number of Burials	76	11
Burials per m³	0.117	0.244
Rooms (Burials in Subfloor Pits)		
Area Excavated	367.6 m²	269.4 m²
Number of Burials	23	1
Burials per m²	0.062	0.004
Number of Rooms Excavated	59	41
Burials per Room	0.390	0.024

27

a single Component II subfloor interment was found, despite the excavation of a large percentage of the known rooms of that period.

Grave accoutrements were associated with more than half the individuals found at Arroyo Hondo. Disregarding the disparity between the sample sizes of the two occupations, 57.4 percent of the Component I graves and 58.3 percent of the Component II graves contained some sort of mortuary item. With regard to skeletal pathologies, again despite the difference between the samples, both components had about the same percentage of individuals exhibiting an observable pathology: Component I, 50.9 percent; Component II, 58.3 percent. The estimated mean height of Component I adults, 159.00 cm, is almost identical to the estimated mean height of Component II adults, 159.55 cm.

3

Population Structure and Nutritional Stress

The survival of any population depends upon its ability to adjust to changing environmental and social conditions. For example, a group practicing subsistence agriculture must adapt to climatic changes to ensure an adequate food supply, especially in a semiarid region such as the American Southwest. An increase in population is another obvious way in which stress might be placed upon resources, demanding a compensating adjustment.

Tree-ring evidence has shown that climate, particularly annual precipitation, has fluctuated throughout the prehistory of the Southwest (Dean and Robinson 1977). Populations have increased, decreased, and shifted their geographic distribution. In the northern Rio Grande region, the years encompassing the occupation of Arroyo Hondo Pueblo saw intervals of above-average rainfall alternating with periods of local or regional drought (Rose, Dean, and Robinson 1979). Furthermore, the late thirteenth and early fourteenth centuries were times of considerable population increase in the northern Rio Grande area (Schoenwetter and Dittert 1968:57).

It is likely that these changes caused some dietary stress among the affected populations. The possible effects of such stress were discussed by Kunitz and Euler (1972:26) in reference to climatic deterioration and population movements in the Southwest during the A.D. 1200s: "In a period when the adult diet was in all probability undergoing a reduction in its protein content, the affects would have been felt most intensely by the youngsters, especially the weanlings. This might well have been reflected in an increase in infant mortality."

In an attempt to determine whether the demographic structure of the Arroyo Hondo population was impacted by dietary stress, two analytical approaches were taken. First, a life table was calculated for the Component I skeletal sample, the only portion of the collection large enough to permit a reliable demographic reconstruction. This life table shows which segments of the population experienced the highest probabilities of death. Second, the skeletal remains were examined for pathologies, particularly those indicated by clinical studies to be related to nutritional deficiencies. The strong association of certain nutrition-related pathologies with the youngest age classes in the skeletal sample suggested that mortality among infants and young children was at least partially a result of dietary stress. It seems likely that either population pressure resulting from the pueblo's rapid growth or climatic deterioration later in its history, or both, created food shortages that affected mortality patterns at Arroyo Hondo.

DEMOGRAPHY

Few attempts have been made to examine systematically the demographic characteristics of prehistoric southwestern populations. Based on his research in the Gran Quivira District, Reed (1967:93) stated, "In the prehistoric Southwest, life expectancy at birth was around 15 years; but only rarely did anyone die near that age. That figure actually represents a combination of a very high infant mortality rate, often approaching 50%, with most deaths later than age three or so falling between 25 and 40."

An examination of the distribution of deaths by age classes at Arroyo Hondo (Table 5) shows a reasonable correspondence between the demographic characteristics of the pueblo and the figures mentioned by Reed. A very high mortality rate is evident among infants and young children at Arroyo Hondo. Due to this high infant mortality, life expectancy at birth was only about 16 years. However, those individuals who survived to the age of 15 could expect to live, on the average, another 19 years. Approximately 58 percent of the population died as subadults. Unfortunately, such comparisons based on the survivorship characteristics of a population are subject to a number of serious biases, among them infant underenumeration and sampling error (Moore, Swedlund, and Armelagos 1975:60–61).

In recent years, demographic methods have been developed that standardize the basic demographic features of prehistoric populations. The life table is a probability model that expresses the mortality and longevity characteristics of a population. Composite life tables are a special case in which calculations are based on skeletal data, specifically the age at death for each individual (Swedlund and Armelagos 1969; Acsádi and Nemeskéri 1970; Weiss 1973; Moore, Swedlund and Armelagos 1975; Palkovich 1978). This kind of table may be used to describe the basic demographic characteristics of a prehistoric population. It represents individuals from an unknown number of generations as a single cohort under the assumption that fluctuations experienced by the population through time, such as changing growth rates, will thus average out. The use of age intervals rather than single-year age classes also acts to smooth fluctuations.

A composite life table was calculated for the 108 individuals associated with the Component I occupation of Arroyo Hondo Pueblo (Table 11). Because the exclusion of individuals in the "adult, age unknown" category would have resulted in the overrepresentation of subadults in the skeletal sample, the age distribution was computed to include all individuals. The proportion of deaths in each adult class (15–19.9 years to 50+ years) was determined, and individuals in the "adult, age unknown" category were distributed according to these proportions (Asch 1976). This corrected age distribution exhibited marked irregularities in the life table (Table 11). Therefore, the values for the number of deaths in each age interval (D_x) were statistically smoothed (Weiss 1973:15) and the composite life table recalculated (Table 12). Smoothing reduces stochastic fluctuations and other inherent errors in the data without masking major perturbations in the age distribution.

The demographic data available for prehistoric periods, based solely on skeletal series, are inherently limited (Palkovich 1978). Recognizing these limitations, Weiss (1973) developed a series of reference model life tables designed specifically to employ anthropological data. These hypothetical mortality schedules, derived by combining a range

31

Ann M. Palkovich

TABLE 11.
Arroyo Hondo composite life table, unsmoothed.

	D_x	d_x	l_x	q_x	L_x	T_x	$\overset{0}{e}_x$	Sq_x^2
0–1	29	26.85	100.00	0.2685	86.58	1667.35	16.67	0.0018
1–4.9	20	18.52	73.15	0.2532	255.56	1580.77	21.61	0.0024
5–9.9	5	4.63	54.63	0.0848	261.58	1325.21	24.26	0.0013
10–14.9	8	7.41	50.00	0.1482	231.48	1063.63	21.27	0.0023
15–19.9	5.75	5.32	42.59	0.1249	199.65	832.15	19.54	0.0024
20–24.9	4.31	3.99	37.27	0.1071	176.38	632.50	16.97	0.0024
25–29.9	4.31	3.99	33.28	0.1199	156.43	456.12	13.71	0.0029
30–34.9	5.75	5.32	29.29	0.1816	133.15	299.69	10.23	0.0047
35–39.9	14.38	13.31	23.97	0.5553	86.58	166.54	6.95	0.0095
40–44.9	2.88	2.67	10.66	0.2505	46.63	79.96	7.50	0.0163
45–49.9	5.75	5.32	7.99	0.6658	26.65	33.33	4.17	0.0258
50+	2.88	2.67	2.67	1.0000	6.68	6.68	2.50	—

KEY

D_x = number of deaths in each age interval

d_x = proportion of deaths in each age interval

$$d_x = \frac{D_x}{\sum\limits_{x=0} D_x}$$

l_x = survivorship for each age interval

$$l_{x+1} = l_x - d_x$$

q_x = probability of death for each age interval

$$q_x = \frac{d_x}{l_x}$$

32

L_x = number of years lived by survivors in each age interval

$$L_x = \frac{n(l_x + l_{x+1})}{2}$$

where n = number of years in each age interval

T_x = total number of years lived by the survivors of each age interval

$$T_x = \sum_{x=0}^{i} L_x$$

$\overset{0}{e}_x$ = life expectancy for each age interval

$$\overset{0}{e}_x = \frac{T_x}{l_x}$$

Sq_x^2 = sample variance for probability of death for each age interval

$$Sq_x^2 = \frac{q_x^2 - (1-q_x)}{D_x}$$

(after Swedlund and Armelagos 1969; Acsádi and Nemeskéri 1979; and Palkovich 1978)

TABLE 12.
Arroyo Hondo composite life table, smoothed.

	D_x	D_x Smoothed	d_x	l_x	q_x	L_x	T_x	$\overset{0}{e}_x$	Sq_x^2
0–1	29	29	26.35	100.00	0.2635	86.83	1623.17	16.23	0.0018
1–4.9	20	18.00	16.35	73.65	0.2220	261.90	1536.34	20.86	0.0021
5–9.9	5	11.00	9.99	57.30	0.1743	261.53	1274.44	22.24	0.0023
10–14.9	8	6.25	5.68	47.31	0.1201	222.35	1012.91	21.41	0.0020
15–19.9	5.75	6.02	5.47	41.63	0.1314	194.48	790.56	18.99	0.0025
20–24.9	4.31	4.79	4.35	36.16	0.1203	169.93	596.08	16.48	0.0027
25–29.9	4.31	4.79	4.35	31.81	0.1367	148.18	426.15	13.40	0.0034
30–34.9	5.75	8.15	7.41	27.46	0.2698	118.78	277.97	10.12	0.0065
35–39.9	14.38	7.67	6.97	20.05	0.3476	82.83	159.19	7.94	0.0103
40–44.9	2.88	7.67	6.97	13.08	0.5329	47.98	76.36	5.84	0.0173
45–49.9	5.75	3.84	3.49	6.11	0.5712	21.83	28.38	4.64	0.364
50+	2.88	2.88	2.62	2.62	1.0000	6.55	6.55	2.50	—

Key: see Table 11.

of adult life expectancy and juvenile mortality values, attempted to establish the underlying age structure characteristics of anthropological populations. The age distribution of deaths in a study population can be compared with Weiss's mortality schedules to determine whether any age classes fail to conform to the range of mortality curves normally exhibited by small-scale human populations. Because q_x, the probability of death, is the only function in the life table that does not exhibit cumulative error from one age category to the next (Moore, Swedlund, and Armelagos 1975:60–61), the q_x values for Arroyo Hondo were compared with those in Weiss's reference model life tables to evaluate the age distribution of deaths in the Arroyo Hondo skeletal sample.

Two of Weiss's tables were selected for comparison, MT:25.0–40.0 and MT:27.5–40.0. Both tables refer to hypothetical mortality schedules in which the juvenile survivorship at age 15 equals 40 out of 100 births. The first table indicates that adult life expectancy at age 15 is 25 years, the second table that adult life expectancy at age 15 is 27.5 years. These tables were selected for comparison with the Arroyo Hondo composite life table since, overall, the q_x values for Arroyo Hondo exhibited the closest match to the q_x values reflected in these reference model life tables.

It is apparent that in general the smoothed q_x values for the Arroyo Hondo population do not exhibit a close correspondence to the q_x values in Weiss's reference model life tables (Fig. 15). While the first five age classes show minor deviations from the expected q_x values, the adult age classes exhibit marked deviations. The 20–24.9 year age class diverges somewhat from the model table with a q_x value lower than the predicted value. However, the sharpest deviation between the Arroyo Hondo and model table values is seen in the adult age categories of 30 years and older. In these age groups, mortality seems to be unusually high at Arroyo Hondo, with q_x values deviating from the reference model life tables earlier in the age distribution than is usually the case in skeletal populations.

The Arroyo Hondo mortality curve might deviate from that of the reference model life tables for any of several reasons, but biases introduced by mortuary practices, biases resulting from aging criteria, and sampling error can probably be ruled out. The prehistoric Pueblos apparently did not spatially segregate their interments by age groups, and so it is unlikely that the age distribution is biased by mortuary

34

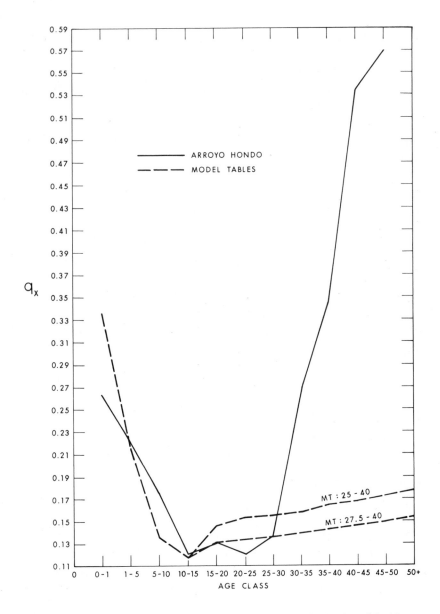

FIG. 15. Comparison of q_x values. Arroyo Hondo smoothed and model tables.

customs. Although biases due to skeletal age criteria, particularly for adults, remain a problem in paleodemographic studies, a wide variety of skeletal studies have yielded demographic results congruent with demographic studies based on other, more reliable sources of data (Weiss 1976:357). Given the standard aging criteria used in this study, it is unlikely that this source of bias has significantly skewed the Arroyo Hondo age distribution. Error related to sample size could only be demonstrated by securing a larger skeletal series from Arroyo Hondo, but samples of at least a hundred individuals are generally considered adequate for paleodemographic studies.

It is clear from the general form of the Arroyo Hondo mortality curve that the first three age classes exhibit high infant/juvenile mortality. Even given the possibility of infant underenumeration, both juvenile survivorship and life expectancy are low, based on composite life table values for these age classes at Arroyo Hondo and comparisons of the probability of death to Weiss's reference model life tables.

The lower than expected probability of death for the 20–24.9 year age group is, at least in part, simply a reflection of the unusually large number of individuals falling into the other adult age classes. However, several other factors might also be responsible for the apparent increased survivorship within this age class. Out-migration from Arroyo Hondo during the later stages of the Component I occupation might have influenced the observed probability of death in the 20–24.9 year age class, at least if the migrants included a significant proportion of young adults. Migration has been noted as playing an important role in the population dynamics at other Pueblo sites (for example, Longacre 1976). Because Weiss's (1973) reference model life tables were designed to represent stationary populations, significant divergences between the model tables and a given study population could also be attributed to population growth or decline through migration, both of which took place at Arroyo Hondo during Component I.

In addition, several recent studies (Lovejoy et al. 1977; Meindl and Swedlund 1977) have suggested that high childhood mortality may result in increased survivorship in subsequent adult age classes. Apparently, those individuals who survive the disease stresses of childhood are biologically best able to cope with disease as young adults. As a result, populations in which mortality is concentrated in the younger age classes may experience increased survivorship among young adults, unlike populations without high levels of childhood mortality. Thus, it

36

is possible that the depressed mortality in the 20–24.9 year age class at Arroyo Hondo may be related to the high childhood mortality.

The great deviation between the q_x values for Arroyo Hondo and those of the reference model life tables for the age classes over 30 years can be attributed, in part, to the relatively large number of accidental deaths falling into these age classes. Nine individuals noted as the victims of accidental deaths fell into four adult age classes: four in the 35–39.9 year class, one each in the 30–34.9 and 45–49.9 year age groups, and three in the "adult, age unknown" class. It is apparent from the mortality curve (Fig. 15) that, particularly for the 35–39.9 year age class, these individuals had a marked impact on the age distribution of deaths in the recovered skeletal sample.

In sum, the general demographic characteristics for the Arroyo Hondo skeletal sample include a high infant/juvenile mortality rate, increased survivorship among young adults, and an unusually high mortality curve among middle and old adult age classes. While biasing factors, such as sampling error, do not appear significantly to affect the Arroyo Hondo age distribution, it seems that some age-specific factors may have affected selected segments of the population.

NUTRITION AND DISEASE

Of the many environmental and cultural factors that can influence mortality patterns, diseases are among the primary determinants. In evaluating the impact of diseases upon mortality schedules, it is crucial to consider the synergistic relationship that frequently exists between disease conditions and nutrition. Dubos (1965:152) stated that "since infection, whatever its causative agent, naturally acts by itself as a form of stress, it thereby tends to aggravate the effect of any underlying quantitative or qualitative protein deficiency." Conversely, malnutrition increases a person's susceptibility to disease. Overlying this biological relationship in human populations is a cultural factor. Social practices, as mechanisms for supplying biological needs, may be directly responsible for disease prevalences or nutritional deficiencies. Again quoting Dubos (1965:147), ". . . inadequacies in the supply or the utilization of food are usually associated with other social or physiological disturbances which may constitute the primary cause of susceptibility to infection."

To evaluate the effects of disease and malnutrition on mortality at Arroyo Hondo Pueblo, the skeletal remains were examined for pathologies that might indicate patterns of disease and nutritional conditions. The reconstruction of nutritional and disease states from skeletal evidence requires careful consideration of the nature of observable pathologies and the range of disease processes that induce such skeletal responses. In many studies, skeletal pathologies have been classified according to general disease categories, a practice that often confuses the description of the pathology with identification of its cause (for example, Miles 1966; Morse 1969; Brothwell 1972). Debate continues about the precise etiologic relationships between particular skeletal conditions and the specific disease processes implied in such classifications. Much research in paleopathology now focuses on differentiating diseases through patterns of skeletal response in individuals—that is, "differential diagnosis." However, it is apparent that many diseases do not elicit skeletal patterns of insult distinguishable from those of other, related diseases. Furthermore, not all diseases leave observable skeletal pathologies, and even when pathologies are present, it is often impossible directly to associate these remnants of disease insult with those conditions that actually brought about the death of the individual.

Because of these problems, the Arroyo Hondo analysis employed categories of pathologies that characterize the actual skeletal conditions rather than attempting to use general disease categories. The pathologies do not reflect the actual causes of death but instead indicate the underlying disease conditions and processes that have left observable effects of insult to the skeletal system. By examining the relationships between the pathology categories and particular age groups, it was possible to establish some of the predominant disease states that affected the Arroyo Hondo population. In some cases, specific pathologies could also be associated with clinically documented disease or nutritional states, allowing more precise effects on mortality patterns to be hypothesized.

The two broadest categories of bone response to disease insult used in this study were osteolysis (softening, resorption, and destruction of osseous tissue) and osteosclerosis (abnormal hardening of bone substance). Within these categories, more specific pathologies could be identified (Tables 13 and 14). Certain skeletal conditions resulting from trauma were also considered. Although accidental death is not actually a skeletal pathology, it was included in the trauma category as

Table 13.
Pathologies observed in the Arroyo Hondo skeletal remains, Component I.

Age Classes	No. of Individuals Per Age Class	OSTEOLYSIS									OSTEOSCLEROSIS			TRAUMA		
		Resorptive Response					Osteolytic Response			Decrease in Bone Density	Increase Bone Mass					
		Localized Resorptive Lesion	Porosity	Endocranial Lesion	Porotic Hyperostosis	Cribra Orbitalia	Localized Periostitis	Widespread Periostitis	Local Osteomyelitis	Bowing	Osteochondroma	Osteoma	Auditory Exostoses	Dislocation	Embedded Projectile Point	Accidental Death
0–1	29	0/18	10/18	5/24	7/24	3/24	0/18	3/18	0/18	1/18	0/18	0/18	0/24	0/18	0/18	0/18
1–4.9	20	0/13	2/13	3/20	3/20	2/20	1/13	0/13	0/13	2/13	0/13	0/13	0/20	0/13	0/13	0/13
5–9.9	5	0/4	0/4	0/4	0/4	0/4	0/4	0/4	0/4	1/4	0/4	0/4	1/4	0/4	0/4	0/4
10–14.9	7	0/6	1/6	0/6	0/6	1/6	1/6	0/6	0/6	1/6	0/6	0/6	0/6	0/6	0/6	0/6
15–19.9	4	0/4	0/4	0/3	0/3	0/4	0/4	0/4	0/4	1/4	0/4	0/4	0/4	0/4	0/4	0/4
20–24.9	3	0/3	0/3	0/3	0/3	0/3	0/3	0/3	1/3	0/3	1/3	0/3	0/3	0/3	0/3	0/3
25–29.9	3	0/3	0/3	0/3	0/3	1/3	0/3	0/3	0/3	2/3	0/3	1/3	0/3	1/3	0/3	0/3
30–34.9	4	0/4	0/4	0/4	0/4	0/4	0/4	0/4	0/4	0/4	0/4	1/4	0/4	0/4	1/4	1/4
35–39.9	10	2/10	0/10	0/8	0/8	0/8	1/10	0/10	0/10	3/10	0/10	0/10	0/8	0/10	0/10	4/10
40–44.9	2	0/2	0/2	0/2	0/2	0/2	0/2	0/2	0/2	1/2	0/2	0/2	0/2	0/2	0/2	0/2
45–49.9	4	0/4	0/4	0/4	0/4	0/4	0/4	0/4	1/4	0/4	0/4	0/4	0/4	0/4	0/4	1/4
50+	2	0/2	0/2	0/1	0/1	0/1	1/2	0/1	0/2	0/2	0/2	0/2	0/1	0/2	0/2	0/2
?	15	0/15	0/15	0/10	0/10	0/10	0/15	0/15	0/15	2/15	0/15	0/15	0/10	0/15	0/15	3/15
Total	108	2/89	13/89	8/93	10/93	7/93	4/89	3/89	2/89	14/89	1/89	2/89	1/93	1/89	1/89	9/89

Number of individuals with pathology/Number of individuals observed.
Missing skeletal parts reduced the number of observations for some skeletal pathologies.

TABLE 14.
Pathologies observed in the Arroyo Hondo skeletal remains, Component II.

Age Classes	No. of Indiv. per age class	OSTEOLYSIS				Decrease Bone Density	OSTEOSCLEROSIS
		Resorptive Response			Osteolytic Response		Increase in Bone Mass
		Endocranial Lesion	Porotic Hyperostosis	Cribra Orbitalia	Localized Periostitis	Bowing	Osteoma
0–1	2	1/2	1/2	2/2	1/2	0/2	0/2
1–4.9	3	0/3	2/3	0/3	0/3	0/3	0/3
5–9.9	1	0/1	1/1	0/1	0/1	—	0/1
10–14.9	0	—	—	—	—	—	—
15–19.9	1	0/1	0/1	0/1	0/1	0/1	0/1
20–24.9	2	0/2	0/1	0/1	0/2	0/2	0/2
25–29.9	0	—	—	—	—	—	—
30–34.9	0	—	—	—	—	—	—
35–39.9	0	—	—	—	—	—	—
40–44.9	1	0/1	0/1	0/1	0/1	1/1	0/1
45–49.9	1	0/1	0/1	0/1	0/1	0/1	0/1
50+	1	0/1	0/1	0/1	0/1	0/1	1/1
?	0	—	—	—	—	—	—
Total	12	1/12	4/11	2/11	1/12	1/11	1/12

Number of individuals with pathology/Number of individuals observed.
Missing skeletal parts reduced the number of observations for some skeletal pathologies.

a cause of death that could be fairly easily identified from the archaeological context of the skeletal remains. Bone conditions resulting from
the degenerative processes of aging or from developmental (genetic)
abnormalities were not included in the analysis because these endoge-
nous disease processes are seldom significant underlying causes of
death. A variety of published descriptions and photographs were used
as standards in identifying skeletal pathologies (see Palkovich 1978).
Patterns of skeletal involvement in pathological responses were evalu-
ated for all individuals in the Arroyo Hondo collection.

Six types of pathology predominated in the Component I skeletal
sample, each appearing in seven or more individuals. All other pathology categories were observed in four or fewer individuals. Among
the predominant pathologies, a group of four classified as resorptive
bone responses within the osteolysis category stand out in their high
incidence within the 0–1 and 1–4.9 year age classes. This group
includes ten cases of porotic hyperostosis (Fig. 16) and eight of endocranial lesions, pathologies involving the destruction of the outer and
inner tables of the cranium, respectively. Both pathologies occurred
exclusively in children under the age of five. Cribra orbitalia, a similar

FIG. 16. An example
of porotic hyperostosis in
a skull fragment from a
child.

41

bone resorption affecting the orbital sockets, appeared in the below-five age groups in five of its seven instances. The fourth pathology in this group, generalized porosity, consists of small, clustered points of cortical bone destruction in the postcranial skeleton. Ten cases of porosity were noted in the 0–1 year class, two in the 1–4.9 year class, and one among the 10–14.9 year subadults.

Bowing of the long bones (Fig. 17), the fifth type of pathology predominant in the Component I sample, occurred throughout the entire range of age classes but was about twice as common among the adults examined as among subadults. Finally, accidental deaths, as mentioned earlier, included only adults over the age of 30 in the School of American Research collection. Of the remaining patholo-gies, a few appeared exclusively in young children (for example, wide-spread periostitis) or in adults (for example, osteoma). However, none of these pathologies were common in the skeletal sample, nor could

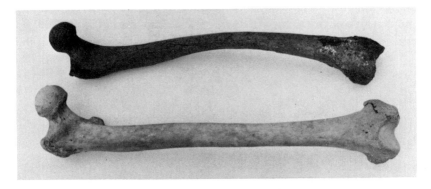

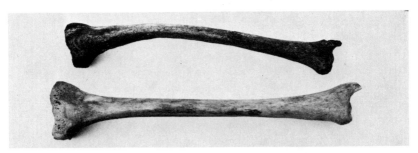

FIG. 17.   Two examples of bowing of the limbs. Bowed specimen on top in each pair, normal bone on bottom. Normal femur 41 cm long.

they be associated with a specific etiologic process likely to alter significantly the age distribution of deaths. The Component II skeletal sample, though very small, exhibited the same general kinds and patterns of pathologies as did the Component I sample.

The association of four clinically related pathologies with the two youngest age groups suggests that these pathologies stemmed from some underlying cause of death that accounted at least partially for the high infant mortality at Arroyo Hondo. Extant populations that show similar patterns of low survivorship in the youngest age classes typically suffer from malnutrition (Wills and Waterloo 1958; Gordon, Wyon, and Ascoli 1967; Puffer and Serrano 1973). Dietary deficiencies may also have been a cause of high infant mortality at Arroyo Hondo, since porotic hyperostosis, endocranial lesions, cribra orbitalia, and general skeletal porosity all have some relationship to nutritional problems (see, for example, Garn 1966; Goldstein 1969; Hengen 1971; Kunitz and Euler 1972; Stini 1973; Lallo, Armelagos, and Mensforth 1977; Mensforth et al. 1978).

Porotic hyperostosis has long been recognized as a pathologic condition in human skeletal remains (Ortner 1975). In his study of skeletons from Pecos Pueblo, Hooton (1930:316– 19) noted 28 cases of this disorder in subadults and young adults. Porotic hyperostosis has been identified elsewhere in New Mexico (Jarcho, Simon, and Jaffe 1965) and in prehistoric pueblos in Arizona (see Zaino 1967, 1968; El-Najjar 1974; El-Najjar, Lozoff, and Ryan 1975; El-Najjar et al. 1976).

In studies of skeletal remains from Arizona and Colorado, Zaino (1967) found an incidence of porotic hyperostosis of about 25 percent over a time span of about 1,300 years. He also measured elemental bone iron in the skeletal series and found that the bone iron content fell within the present-day normal range. From these observations, Zaino concluded that the Anasazi Indians of Pueblo II times in Arizona had a nutritionally adequate diet and that porotic hyperostosis was "most likely a sign of severe fatal congenital hemolytic anemia such as thalassemia. Nutrition alone appears to be an unlikely cause" (1967:42).

Zaino's conclusions, however, have been contested by Kunitz and Euler (1972). They point out that a 25 percent incidence rate is extremely high for a congenital defect. With such high incidence prehistorically, the defect should still be present in extant populations, yet it is absent in living Pueblo groups. Kunitz and Euler (1972:32) suggest that the entity known as symmetrical osteoporosis or spongy hyperostosis is in the majority of cases likely to be due to iron deficiency anemia as a result of prolonged breast feeding without supplemental iron. It is possible that it acted synergistically with the entity that has come to be known as "weanling diarrhea" in causing a high infant mortality rate. (1972:32)

Research by El-Najjar (1974; El-Najjar, Lozoff, and Ryan 1975; El-Najjar et al. 1976), although based on isolated cases, supports the view that porotic hyperostosis in the Southwest may be caused by iron deficiency anemia. Other studies also mention iron deficiency anemia as a possible causative agent of this pathology (Hengen 1971; Carlson, Armelagos, and Van Gervan 1974).

If prehistoric Pueblo populations did suffer from such anemia, one of its major causes was likely the insufficient absorption of dietary iron attributable to a predominance of maize, an inhibitor to absorption of dietary iron, in the diet (El-Najjar 1977). Since infants and young children are more sensitive than adults to dietary or disease stress, these young age classes are the first to show the effects of, and suffer the most severe responses to, such stress. However, why hyperostosis and related skeletal manifestations of malnutrition are found predominantly among juveniles has not been established.

Support for the view that hyperostosis is caused by iron anemia occurring mostly among infants and young children can be found in an ethnographic account of infant diet and feeding habits among the Hopis (Dennis 1940). At the town of Hotevilla, infants were predominantly breast-fed until around one year of age, their diet sometimes supplemented with foods high in carbohydrates, such as cornmeal and tortillas, or by chili (Aberle 1932:339; Dennis 1940:34). Mother's milk is low in dietary iron; therefore, prolonged breast-feeding may lead to anemia. Dennis also noted (1940:34) that the high infant mortality rate at Hotevilla was apparently due to digestive disturbances, which were common in early childhood. Childhood deaths due to diarrhea have been linked in some instances to various anemic conditions (Puffer and Serrano 1973). If prolonged breast-feeding of infants was practiced at Arroyo Hondo, where corn was probably a major part of the diet and where food shortages probably accompanied intervals of local drought (Wetterstrom 1976:56), then iron deficiency anemia may have been an important underlying cause of infant deaths.

Endocranial lesions, cribra orbitalia, and generalized skeletal porosity have been noted in other populations also exhibiting hyperostosis (for example, Angel 1971; Lallo, Armelagos, and Mensforth 1977). In such populations, these four pathologies seem to manifest themselves as variable responses to nutritional stress among individuals younger than five years of age at death. Individuals exhibit various stages of pathological severity, with different combinations of the pathologies manifested in any one individual (hyperostosis usually being the most frequent pathology). While the precise etiologic relationship between hyperostosis and the other pathologies has not yet been established, it is clear from clinical research and studies of extant and prehistoric populations that all of these skeletal manifestations are related to a synergism between malnutrition and infectious disease states.

The incidence of these four pathologies among individuals younger than five years of age at Arroyo Hondo suggests that infants and young children were severely affected by iron deficiency anemia, which might have represented a more general state of malnutrition in the entire population. Thus weakened, the infants were more susceptible to a variety of diseases that themselves acted synergistically with the nutritional stress. The skeletal evidence, therefore, suggests that high infant mortality at Arroyo Hondo was at least partially attributable to a combination of poor nutrition and related childhood diseases.

Bowing of the long bones, a common pathology among adults at Arroyo Hondo, was probably not directly related to an immediate cause of death, but it may have been another effect of dietary deficiencies. Although bowing was found only in the major long bones, the skeletons of the affected individuals generally exhibited less mineralization and thinner cortexes than does normal bone. Given the occurrence of bowing in all age categories and throughout the occupational span of Arroyo Hondo, a genetic or developmental basis for the condition seems unlikely. Instead, bowing may have been produced by a dietary deficiency of minerals essential for bone maintenance. Although the observed pattern of involvement at Arroyo Hondo did not precisely correspond to the pattern usually associated with inadequate bone mineralization in adults, termed osteomalacia (Aegerter and Kirkpatrick 1968; Jaffe 1972; Steinbock 1976), it is still possible that this condition was a residual effect of dietary stress experienced at an earlier age by the affected individuals. Bowing, therefore, is probably not indicative of a disease condition that influenced adult mortality but, rather, reflects the same childhood malnutrition that helped to account for low survivorship in the younger age classes.

In another, independent study (Palkovich 1978), the author assessed the skeletal pathology patterns delimited by differential diagnosis by examining the statistical associations between skeletal pathology incidence and age class in the Arroyo Hondo skeletal sample. Results of an analysis of variance showed that pathologies clinically associated with iron deficiency anemia (porotic hyperostosis, cribra orbitalia, endocranial lesions, etc.) generally fell within the appropriate predicted age range of 1–4.9 years. This analysis yielded a high statistical association between the age distribution and certain age-specific skeletal pathologies. In addition, a principal component analysis showed significant statistical correlations among the nutrition-related skeletal pathologies, which accounted for the majority of the explained variance in the age distribution (Palkovich 1978:211–18). In general, these statistical analyses corroborate the association among several age-specific pathologies observed clinically to result from malnutrition and associated infectious disease processes and also suggest that deviations observed in the mortality profile for Arroyo Hondo are associated with increased mortality/morbidity in those age classes affected by particular disease processes (Palkovich 1978:222–23). A detailed analysis of the relationship of mortality patterns to disease processes for the Arroyo Hondo population may be found in Palkovich (1978).

CONCLUSIONS

A composite life table calculated for the Component I occupation of Arroyo Hondo Pueblo exhibited a mortality profile with three distinct features: high mortality among infants and young children; low probability of death among young adults; and a level of mortality among middle and old adults that was unusually high when compared with reference model life tables developed by Weiss (1973). A variety of factors may be responsible for the low mortality among young adults. The unexpected distribution of deaths in the older adult age classes may be partly attributable to the relatively large number of accidental deaths represented in the skeletal sample, all of which clustered in the age groups over 30.

An examination of skeletal pathologies in the Arroyo Hondo collection demonstrated that a group of four pathologies, all involving the resorption and destruction of osseous tissue, were strongly associated with the 0–1 year and 1–4.9 year age classes. Each of these pathologies has a clinically documented occurrence with malnutrition, specifically iron deficiency anemia. Therefore, it is suggested that malnutrition, acting in combination with infectious disease, was at least partially responsible for the high level of mortality among infants and young children at Arroyo Hondo. The malnutrition and related disease conditions themselves may have been the results of infant diet and feeding practices, a general emphasis on high-carbohydrate foods, and/or periodic food shortages caused by local drought.

4

Mortuary Practices: Test of an Ethnographic Age-Status Model

The mortuary practices of a prehistoric society, observed as patterns of burials, can provide valuable information about the group's ceremonial and social organization. Both Saxe (1970) and Binford (1971) point out that the differential mortuary treatment of individuals is a direct reflection of each person's cumulative social position, including age, sex, or other status criteria, at the time of death. Studies such as those by Brown (1971) and Saxe (1970) have attempted to use this important source of information about prehistoric societies.

Most discussions of Pueblo mortuary practices have focused on specific, ethnographically known details. However, many aspects of present-day Pueblo ceremonies are products of the combining of traditional Pueblo and introduced Christian rites and therefore do not lend themselves to use in ethnographic analogy. Other features, though, are distinctly traditional. Among the more extensive reviews of these mortuary practices are those by Parsons (1929, 1939), Eggan (1950), Ellis

49

(1968), and Ortiz (1969). Ellis, in particular, emphasizes the aspects of burial rites that leave recoverable remains to which prehistoric material might be compared for evidence of parallel or similar behavior. Because of the cultural continuity between prehistoric and modern Pueblo groups, it seems reasonable that correlations between historically observed customs and certain archaeological finds be proposed and tested.

Though mortuary practices vary among the modern Pueblos, certain features are said to be found in most groups. Generally, the body is interred with its head to the east, the direction in which the individual's journey to the underworld begins (Parsons 1939:70,72; Ellis 1968:65). Items buried with adults are usually those that the individual once owned (Ortiz 1969:51–52). All clothing is torn and reversed, as are other items, symbolizing the reversed nature of the spirit world (Ellis 1968:65,71; Ortiz 1969:50). A bowl and some food may be placed with the individual for the journey to the underworld, the bowl being broken first and the food placed on the left side or in the left armpit (Ellis 1968:63). Infants may be treated slightly differently than adults. Several accounts indicate that the young may be interred under the floor of a room (White 1962:202; 1942:178; Ellis 1968:67). According to Parsons (1939:71), this is because "The spirit of the uninitiated Hopi child lingers about the house until it is reborn to its mother or until she dies, a belief in child reincarnation as held at Cochiti and Jemez."

In some ways, the Arroyo Hondo mortuary remains parallel the ethnographic descriptions. Evidence of food, primarily corn and squash, was found with a number of individuals, as were utilitarian and decorative items that could have been the deceased's personal possessions. More than one-third of the burials were oriented with their heads to the east. On the other hand, the uniformity of certain practices suggested by the ethnographic accounts was certainly not seen at Arroyo Hondo. This uniformity itself may be more a result of a desire to generalize about varied customs than a reflection of consistency in practice.

At the same time, variability in the archaeological remains may be caused by many factors. For example, the fact that food items were not universally found might be because of differential preservation. Variability might also be explained by the existence of a range of accepted practices. Perhaps in some cases food was symbolically represented by

cornmeal (Ortiz 1969:23), which decomposes quickly. That head orientation need not always be to the east is suggested by Ortiz's note
(1969:52) that "after the soul is released from the body through the
mouth, it is believed to go immediately to one of the four directional
shrines." These examples indicate that simple comparisons with ethnographic descriptions can sometimes be more confusing than informative.

A more systematic approach to examining the correlations between
prehistoric and historic Pueblo mortuary activities was that of Clark
(1969). In his work on Grasshopper Pueblo, a prehistoric western
Pueblo site, he attempted to construct a model of mortuary behavior
and to test its implications for the archaeologically recovered mortuary
remains. Clark considered kinship, territoriality, sodalities, and stratification as alternative forms of social organization that might be reflected
in the burial clusters at Grasshopper. He found that "evidence for
social stratification was abundant. It suggests that status was ascribed at
birth through membership in kin groupings" (Clark 1969:1).

Clark also suggested that a form of age grading may have been a
significant feature of the prehistoric social organization at Grasshopper
Pueblo. Noting that "western Pueblo society is characterized by a whole
series of . . . transition rites, extending from those concerned with
birth (such as naming and clan initiation) to those conferring adult
status" (1969:20), he goes on to assert that

> It is possible that specific kinds of artifacts may be found with
> burials of specific ages. This would point to an elaboration of
> passage rites analogous to the modern Western Pueblos, constitut-
> ing, in effect, a system of age-grading which would be reflected in
> the burial population. More precisely, individuals of one age-set
> would be characterized by different ornaments or pottery from
> those of another age-set, indicating their relative statuses in the
> age-grading system. (1969:26)

Clark also noted that the social organization evident at Grasshopper
appeared to be "a much more elaborate development of stratification
than is present in the modern Western Pueblos" (1969:26–27).

It is possible that a similar age-grading system was practiced by the
prehistoric eastern Pueblos as well. To investigate this possibility, the
mortuary remains from Arroyo Hondo were examined in light of Ortiz's

51

(1969) ethnographically based model of the age-grading system of the present-day eastern Pueblos.

THE AGE-STATUS MODEL

The present-day Tewas, of the eastern Pueblo linguistic groups, provide a model of a social organization that includes various status levels or grades based on age and position within the ceremonial hierarchy. As described by Ortiz (1969), a Tewa individual passes through at least six formal rites of passage (Table 15). Four of the rites take place when the person reaches certain ages; the fifth is the marriage ceremony, performed any time during adulthood; and the final rite is performed at death. Children under the age of six are said to be "unripe" because they have not yet passed through the water-pouring ceremony by which they become fully established as common Tewas (Ortiz 1969:37). For this rite, "the upper age is not a rigid limit, but the lower one is; that is to say, the child must be at least six years of age" (Ortiz 1969:37).

Adult Tewas can aspire to several status positions within the political and religious structure. The *Towa'e*, or political officials, and the *Oxua*, those who impersonate the deities during rituals, undergo no formal rites of passage and at death are buried like any ordinary member of the society (Ortiz 1969:96). The *Patowa*, or "Made People," must pass through a series of rites that makes them representatives of the deities and full members of the ritual society. At death they are distinguished "in that the survivors of the deceased's society paint the corpse in a process called 'marking him to become Oxua'. . . . The ritual objects owned by a Made Person may not be used again, and these are retired to a lake or mountain shrine" (Ortiz 1969:96). Finally, the *Sehshu* are lay assistants to the *Patowa* and like them are marked at death to join the deities. Except for the *Oxua*, whose membership is restricted to males, all status positions may be attained by both men and women.

Three major levels of being, then, are found in present-day Tewa social organization: children below the age of six, common members of the society (those over six years of age), and among the adults, those who are members of ritual societies. Using these levels as a general model of the eastern Pueblo age- and status-grading system, it was

52

TABLE 15.
Tewa age grades and acquired statuses, summarized from Ortiz (1969).

Age	Rite	Name of Status	Description of Status
Newborn	—	Ochu ("Unripe")	Unincorporated into society; not yet Tewa or human.
Four days	Naming	Ochu	Identified as a member of Tewa society at large.
During first year	"Water-giving"	Ochu	Associated with father's moiety, into which recruitment begins.
6–10 years (at least 6)	"Water-pouring"	Seh't'a ("Dry Food")	Common Tewa; is assigned sex-specific tasks and behavior.
Early teens (at least 10)	"Finishing"	Seh't'a	Adult member of moiety; can participate in ritual activities and is eligible to become Patowa.
Adult	Marriage	Seh't'a	Fully incorporated into Tewa society and moieties; men eligible to become Towa'e.
Adult	—	Towa'e ("Of the Middle of the Structure")	Political official; temporary position of authority as mediator within society.
Adult	—	Oxua ("Cloud Beings")	Impersonator of deities (Oxua) during moiety rituals; at death, retains "Dry Food Person" status.
Adult	"Life-breath-blow blessing"	Sehshu	Lay assistant to the "Made People"; retains status of "Dry Food Person" in life, but "marked" like "Made Person" at death to become Oxua.
Adult	Series of rites	Patowa ("Made People")	Representative of the deities; acts as intermediary between secular and supernatural; has access to all ritual knowledge and prerogatives; joins the mythical Oxua at death.
At death	"Releasing"	—	Same as that at time of death, but has been given passage to the underworld.

hypothesized that Arroyo Hondo Pueblo maintained a similar form of organization that would be reflected in its mortuary remains. Different kinds of burial treatment and grave accoutrements were expected to be seen among the individuals belonging to the different age or status positions.

TESTING THE IMPLICATIONS OF THE MODEL

Two approaches, one quantitative and the other qualitative, were taken in testing the archaeological implications of the ethnographic model. First, statistical tests were used to look for correlations between age groups and variables of grave location and accoutrements. Second, the kinds of grave goods and other attributes of adult burials were examined to determine whether some adults had received the special treatment considered characteristic of ceremonial status. Because of the small burial sample dating to the Component II occupation of Arroyo Hondo, only the mortuary data of Component I were used in the analysis. The results of the study tended to support the prediction that at least three age-status classes were recognized by the people of Arroyo Hondo.

Tests for Evidence of Age Grading

Two statistical tests, both standard for use with nominal data, were chosen to test the significance of the mortuary remains in terms of the age-grade model. Various categories of data recorded for each burial, such as location, types of grave accoutrements, and age were treated as nominal scales. The chi-square test (Walker and Lev 1953:95–108; Blalock 1972:275–314) examines the degree of relationship between nominal classes of data in a cross-classified, contingency table format. In this case, the null hypothesis predicts that no statistically significant relationship exists between age groups and classes of mortuary data. The Kolmogorov-Smirnov (K-S) two-sample test (Siegel 1956:127–36; Blalock 1972:262–65) examines the statistical significance of the difference between the cumulative frequencies of two samples. Like the chi-square test, the Kolmogorov-Smirnov test was used to identify possible correlations between age classes and categories of mortuary data. Again, the null hypothesis predicts that no statistically significant

54

TABLE 16.
Chi-square test of general age groups and burial locations.

	Subadult	Adult	Total
Rooms	18	5	23
Plazas and Trash	44	32	76
Total	62	37	99

$X^2 = 3.129$
Approximate level of significance = 0.10

relationships exist among the variables of age, location, and grave goods. Both the chi-square and the K-S two-sample tests employ a chi-square distribution in establishing levels of significance. Each test was run on all possible combinations of variables in the Component I data, but only the results found most informative or relevant to the study are presented here.

Tests were first run on burial location and orientation. The results of a simple chi-square test for relationships between age categories (adult and subadult) and location (rooms and plazas/trash) were not significant at the 0.01 level (Table 16). A series of K-S two-sample tests employing the chi-square distribution as a measure of significance showed no significant differences between subadults and adults with respect either to location or to orientation of the head (Table 17). Thus, in terms of these variables, there seems to have been no mortuary distinction made between individuals of the two broad age categories. In addition, the ethnographically recorded practice of burying infants beneath the floors of rooms was paralleled at Arroyo Hondo in only 31 percent of the cases of children less than one year old.

TABLE 17.
Kolmogorov-Smirnov tests of general age groups, head orientations, and burial locations.

DATA SET							
	PLAZAS				ROOMS		
	Subadult	Adult	Total		Subadult	Adult	Total
N	11	2	13	N	3	0	3
S	7	6	13	S	2	1	3
E	16	11	27	E	6	1	7
W	6	3	9	W	2	2	4
?	4	10	14	?	5	1	6
Total	44	32	76	Total	18	5	23

TABLE 17. (continued)

K-S TESTS
(Numbers and proportions are cumulative.)

					Greatest Difference	χ^2	Approximate Level of Significance
PLAZAS							
	Subadult		*Adult*				
N	11	0.275	2	0.091	0.184	1.92	0.20
S	18	0.450	8	0.364			
E	34	0.850	19	0.864			
W	40	1.000	22	1.000			
ROOMS							
	Subadult		*Adult*				
N	3	0.231	0	0.000			
S	5	0.385	1	0.250			
E	11	0.846	2	0.500	0.346	1.46	0.30
W	13	1.000	4	1.000			
COMBINED AGE GROUPS							
	Plazas		*Rooms*				
N	13	0.210	3	0.176			
S	26	0.419	6	0.353			
E	53	0.855	13	0.765	0.090	0.432	0.55
W	62	1.000	17	1.000			
SUBADULTS							
	Plazas		*Rooms*				
N	11	0.275	3	0.231			
S	18	0.450	5	0.385	0.065	0.166	0.70
E	34	0.850	11	0.846			
W	40	1.000	13	1.000			
ADULTS							
	Plazas		*Rooms*				
N	2	0.091	0	0.000			
S	8	0.364	1	0.250			
E	19	0.864	2	0.500	0.364	1.79	0.20
W	22	1.000	4	1.000			
COMBINED PROVENIENCES							
	Subadult		*Adult*				
N	14	0.264	2	0.077	0.187	2.440	0.30
S	23	0.434	9	0.346			
E	45	0.849	21	0.808			
W	53	1.000	26	1.000			

TABLE 18.
Kolmogorov-Smirnov test of age groups and common grave goods.

Age in Years	Presence of Blanket or Mat		Absence of Blanket or Mat		Greatest Difference
0–1	17	0.405	12	0.235	
1–4.9	29	0.690	20	0.392	0.298
5–9.9	31	0.738	23	0.451	
10–14.9	33	0.786	28	0.549	
15–19.9	34	0.810	31	0.608	
20–24.9	34	0.810	34	0.667	
25–29.9	36	0.857	35	0.686	
30–34.9	37	0.881	38	0.745	
35–39.9	38	0.905	47	0.922	
40–44.9	40	0.952	47	0.922	
45–49.9	41	0.976	50	0.980	
50+	42	1.000	51	1.000	

$X^2 = 8.18$
Approximate level of significance = 0.02

The next category of mortuary data to be considered was that of grave accoutrements. A K-S two-sample test of the most common grave goods— hide blankets and yucca-fiber mats—indicated a significant difference between the various age classes in terms of the presence or absence of these items (Table 18). A simple chi-square test of the presence or absence of blankets and mats among adults and subadults produced similar results (Table 19).

Because 75 percent of the hide blankets and yucca mats had been found with subadults, it was decided to divide the population into age groups cross-cutting that category. In keeping with the prediction of the model that children under age six made up a separate status group, a K-S two-sample test was run using the age groups 0–6 years and 6.1–50+ years. A significant difference was obtained at the 0.001

TABLE 19.
Chi-square test of general age groups and common grave goods.

	Subadult	Adult	Total
Presence of Blanket or Mat	33	11	44
Absence of Blanket or Mat	29	26	55
Total	62	37	99

$X^2 = 5.18$
Approximate level of significance = 0.03

TABLE 20.

Kolmogorov-Smirnov test of adjusted age groups and common grave goods.

	0–6 Years		6.1–50+ Years		Greatest Difference
Blanket	23	0.315	6	0.128	
Mat	40	0.548	14	0.298	
Both	50	0.685	14	0.298	0.387
Neither	73	1.000	47	1.000	

$X^2 = 17.127$
Approximate level of significance = 0.001

level (Table 20). However, when the 0–6 year age category was further broken down, significant differences were not found in the occurrence of blankets and mats. This finding suggests that mortuary treatment of children under six years old was significantly different from that of older individuals but no distinctions were made within the 0–6 year age class. Older children and adults were sometimes wrapped in hides or placed on yucca-fiber mats for burial, but the practice was significantly more common among the younger children.

Two other kinds of grave accoutrements—sherds and infrequently occurring items—were subjected to statistical tests. The category "sherds" includes both whole pots and pottery fragments. Infrequently occurring items are those that were rare or unique in the collection, such as shells, wooden objects, feathers, jet, turquoise, and bone artifacts. Because more than one item was recovered with some individuals, distinctions were made between the number of individuals having one or more items and those with none. Simple chi-square tests indicate no significant differences between subadults and adults in the occurrence of sherds or rare items (Tables 21 and 22). When the age classes of 0–6 years and 6.1–50+ years were used, no significant differences were found in the presence or absence of pottery (Table 23). However, a comparable test of rare items showed that although such goods did appear with children under six years of age, they were significantly more often associated with older individuals (Table 24). This distribution coincides with the hypothesized status distinction between individuals above and below six years of age. However, it also suggests that some individuals younger than six years may have had ascribed statuses that are reflected in the rare items buried with them.

TABLE 21.

Chi-square test of general age groups and pottery.

	Subadult	Adult	Total
Presence of Sherd or Pot	8	4	12
Absence of Sherd or Pot	54	33	87
Total	62	37	99

$X^2 = 0.095$
Approximate level of significance = 0.75

TABLE 22.

Chi-square test of general age groups and infrequently occurring grave goods.

	Subadult	Adult	Total
Presence of Rare Item	12	12	24
Absence of Rare Item	50	25	75
Total	62	37	99

$X^2 = 2.158$
Approximate level of significance = 0.15

TABLE 23.

Chi-square test of adjusted age groups and pottery.

	0–6 Years	6.1–50+ Years	Total
Presence of Sherd or Pot	6	6	12
Absence of Sherd or Pot	56	31	87
Total	62	37	99

$X^2 = 0.930$
Approximate level of significance = 0.40

TABLE 24.

Chi-square test of adjusted age groups and infrequently occurring grave goods.

	0–6 Years	6.1–50+ Years	Total
Presence of Rare Item	9	15	24
Absence of Rare Item	53	22	75
Total	62	37	99

$X^2 = 8.545$
Approximate level of significance = 0.01

Evidence of Ceremonial Statuses

A qualitative assessment of the grave accoutrements and body treatment seen in the Arroyo Hondo burials provided evidence for special ceremonial statuses among the adults. Three individuals in particular

59

stood out from the overall pattern of adult interment. Two of these were the only adult males found in subfloor pits in rooms, and the third was a female also buried beneath a floor. One of the males (specimen 12-16-36-4-1) was about 44 years old at the time of death, and the female (specimen 12-16-29-5-1) was a few years older. Both exhibited the remains of paint that had been applied to their bodies before burial. Red ochre adhered to the feet and legs of the female, yellow and white pigment to the face, arms, and legs of the male (Fig. 18).

It is possible, of course, that other individuals at Arroyo Hondo had been painted before burial but the pigments simply were not preserved or recovered. Still, body painting seems to have been rare and suggests that the two individuals just described held special status positions in life. The practice is also strikingly similar to the painting of the corpses of "Made People" mentioned by Ortiz (1969:96), a parallel that implies a ritual basis for the status distinction.

The other unusual male burial (specimen 12-19-1-V-1) was an individual about 25 years old at the time of death. Interred with him

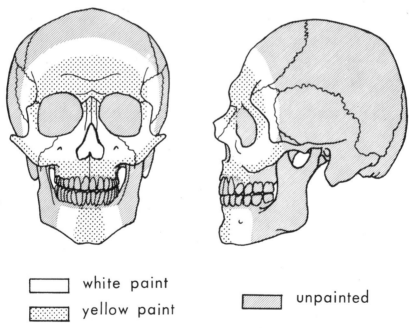

white paint

yellow paint

unpainted

FIG. 18.   Distribution of paint on face of burial 12-16-36-4-1.

were the greatest number and variety of grave goods found with any one burial at Arroyo Hondo (Fig. 19). In the area of the knees were the skin of a common raven, the wings of a white-necked raven, four stone arrowpoints, some wood fragments possibly representing a bow, seven stone balls, a small stone square, and the claw of an eagle. Near the occipital lay a bone awl tip and two sheets of mica with paired, drilled holes. These items may have been part of a headdress or hair ornament.

Both the large collection of rare items and the fact that this individual was one of only two male subfloor burials suggest that he too had acquired some special status in life. Certain of his grave accoutrements resemble those of a deceased "medicine man" described by Ellis (1968:64):

> The deposit for a medicine man may include two baskets, each holding a pair of eagle feather exorcisors, a bear or eagle claw necklace from which dangles a crystal used in locating or diagnosing a disease, a bracelet of strung olivella shells among which a few stone arrowpoints are tied, and perhaps a headband. These all are personally owned bits of ceremonial equipment.

By analogy, the Arroyo Hondo individual might have held a similar sort of ritual position.

Nearly all other grave accoutrements found with adults at Arroyo Hondo could be construed as ordinary personal possessions. Two exceptions were a clay pipe or cloud blower and a stone axe painted with red and white pigments, both found with adult males. These items might have been pieces of ritual paraphernalia.

The grave goods most commonly accompanying subadults were body wrappings and food offerings. However, two children under the age of six were found with rather elaborate necklaces of stone and shell, and a third was buried with a pine branch on which were four bone tubes and a stone cylinder. Assuming a subadult probably could not have earned such rare items on his own, these items suggest that certain individuals were afforded some form of status ascription similar to that noted by Clark (1969:30) for Grasshopper Pueblo. On the other hand, it is also possible that these items were ritual paraphernalia associated with a particular age-grade status. Ortiz (1969:31) noted that among the eastern Pueblos, shell, stone axes, arrowpoints, and lightning stones are ceremonial items associated with the naming ritual.

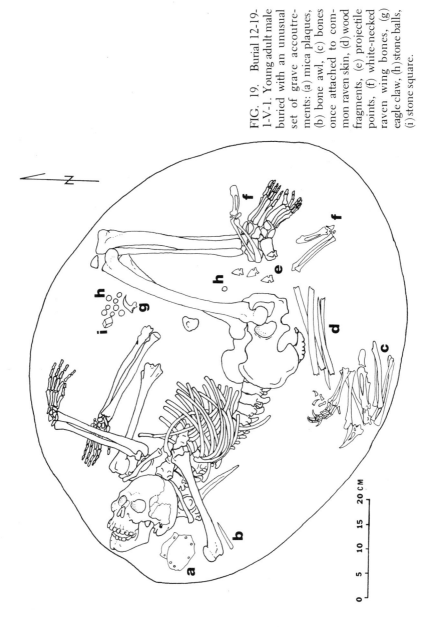

FIG. 19. Burial 12-19-1V-1. Young adult male buried with an unusual set of grave accoutrements: (a) mica plaques, (b) bone awl, (c) bones once attached to common raven skin, (d) wood fragments, (e) projectile points, (f) white-necked raven wing bones, (g) eagle claw, (h) stone balls, (i) stone square.

62

Other symbolism is attached to specific items; for example, "spruce and fir branches are used in ritual the whole year round . . ." (Ortiz 1969:94). Such items might have been buried with an individual who had just experienced or was about to experience a rite of passage to another age-grade status at the time of death.

CONCLUSIONS

The analysis of Arroyo Hondo mortuary practices tends to support the hypothesis that a system of age and ceremonial status grading was in effect at the pueblo, as it is today among eastern Pueblo communities. The model of Tewa status organization derived from Ortiz (1969) included three general age-status grades: (1) those six years of age or less, who are not yet fully incorporated into the society, (2) those over the age of six, who are common members of the society, and (3) adults who possess ceremonial knowledge and provide special ritual services to the community.

Statistical tests showed that at Arroyo Hondo, children under the age of six were significantly more often wrapped in hide blankets and/or laid on yucca-fiber mats for burial than were adults. They were significantly less often accompanied by rare or unusual grave goods than were older individuals. These findings indicate that young children were indeed treated differently than adults upon burial, and therefore it is inferred that the 0–6 year age class was recognized as a separate status group by the Arroyo Hondo inhabitants.

Among the adult burials, three individuals who exhibited unusual body treatment or grave accoutrements served as evidence of a distinction between ordinary members of the society and those holding special ceremonial status. The body paint of two of these individuals and some of the artifacts accompanying the third have close parallels among the ethnographically recorded grave accoutrements of persons known to have had ritual positions.

Finally, this age-grade system may also have included some kind of status ascription, particularly for subadults, through kinship. Such an elaboration of the basic age-grade system is not evident in historic and recent eastern Pueblo social organization. This possible prehistoric status ascription parallels a similar elaboration of an age-grade system that Clark (1969) noted for prehistoric western Pueblo groups.

5

Summary and Comparisons

The preceding chapters presented basic data about the Arroyo Hondo skeletal and mortuary remains and described analyses pertaining to demography and social organization. In summarizing the information and results of the analyses, it is useful to compare them with data from other Pueblo sites in the northern Rio Grande region to see whether Arroyo Hondo fits the general demographic and mortuary pattern of the area. Because no comprehensive survey of skeletal and mortuary data from the northern Rio Grande region was available, the author reviewed the literature concerning five sites that were occupied during approximately the same time period as Arroyo Hondo Pueblo. These five were the only contemporaneous sites for which adequate information for the purposes of this study has been published. Unpublished field notes were also available in most cases but were not used in this study. The sites selected for comparison were Forked Lightning and Pecos Pueblo, located in the upper Pecos River drainage; Paa-ko, situated on the eastern slope of the Sandia Mountains; Pindi Pueblo, on the Santa Fe River; and the Alfred Herrera site, on the Rio Grande (Map 1).

The available site reports were not strictly comparable either among themselves or with Arroyo Hondo because they present data in different ways and in varying degrees of completeness. Field strategies at the other sites differed from that at Arroyo Hondo by heavily emphasizing room excavation, a practice that to some extent might have introduced biases into age profiles, sex distribution, occurrence of grave goods, and so forth. In reporting grave accoutrements, all items recovered with a skeleton in a formal grave at Arroyo Hondo were listed, but at other sites, items such as blankets or mats were not always counted as grave goods. Differential preservation of bone and perishable artifacts is another factor to be considered. For all these reasons, comparisons among the sites could not be entirely systematic, and caution must be exercised in evaluating the variability between them.

The occupation dates of each of the comparative sites are based on those originally provided by the authors of the various reports but have been modified by Richard W. Lang (n.d.), who reviewed the ceramic and tree-ring evidence from each site as part of his analysis of the Arroyo Hondo pottery. Forked Lightning, the earliest of the sites, was a pueblo of approximately 150 rooms. Using a ceramic chronology, Stubbs (in Kidder 1958:42) placed the founding of the site at about A.D. 1250 and its abandonment at A.D. 1300. Lang, however, dates the establishment of Forked Lightning between the A.D. 1220s and 1250 and the abandonment in the A.D. 1320s. Most excavation at Forked Lightning was conducted in roomblocks, and 152 single-burial graves were uncovered (Kidder 1958:28).

Pindi Pueblo (LA 1) is a site of at least 300 rooms surrounding several plaza areas. Stubbs and Stallings (1953:23) estimated that Pindi was occupied between A.D. 1250 and 1348, while Lang suggests a span from about A.D. 1270 to 1350–65. Here too excavation was conducted primarily in rooms, yielding 90 individuals, 86 of them from formal graves.

At the site of Paa-ko (LA 162), which consisted of two building clusters comprising well over 800 rooms, occupation took place during both the prehistoric and historic periods. The prehistoric interval, dated by Lambert (1954:174) from about A.D. 1300 to 1425, was closely contemporaneous with the habitation of Arroyo Hondo Pueblo. Excavation, mainly in roomblocks, produced 146 individuals, 16 of them in a mass grave.

Pecos Pueblo (LA 625), a major site in the northern Rio Grande region, was a multistoried pueblo containing hundreds of rooms. Occupied from about A.D. 1300 until well into the historic period, only its earliest two time periods are of interest in this study. Kidder's Black-on-white period is roughly contemporaneous with Component I at Arroyo Hondo, his Glaze I period with Component II (Richard W. Lang: personal communication). Most excavation at Pecos took place in roomblocks and trash middens. At least 1,938 individuals were recovered from the pueblo (Kidder 1958:279), but only the 573 found with datable decorated pottery were studied and reported. Given that the frequency of skeletal and mortuary characteristics for this site is based on only a portion of the burials with decorated sherds and less than 30 percent of the total number of burials recovered, the reported frequency data for Pecos are undoubtedly skewed and unrepresentative of this population.

Finally, the Alfred Herrera site, reported by Lange and others (1968), was a small pueblo of approximately 80 rooms. The Eastern Sector of the site, in which about half of the rooms were semisubterranean, was occupied from about A.D. 1350 to 1425 (Honea in Lange 1968:163, 166), making it roughly contemporaneous with Component II at Arroyo Hondo. Excavation took place predominantly in rooms, yielding a total of 54 interments.

SUMMARY AND COMPARISON OF MORTUARY DATA

Burial Locations

The people of Arroyo Hondo Pueblo buried their dead in a variety of locations throughout all parts of the town. Plaza surfaces contained 50.5 percent of all formal burials found during excavation, trash deposits in plazas and abandoned rooms accounted for 27.9 percent, and subfloor pits in rooms held 21.6 percent. Comparable statistics cannot be compiled for other sites in the northern Rio Grande region because excavation strategies differed among them. However, the same general kinds of locations are repeated elsewhere. For example, at Pindi Pueblo, Stubbs and Stallings found that "refuse deposits held 38 percent, abandoned rooms 29 percent and sub-floor pits 25 percent" of all individuals (1953:143). Paa-ko burials were "practically all . . . located below room floors and in refuse filling rooms" (Lambert 1954:164). The

Alfred Herrera site produced 31 burials in pit rooms, 21 in the kiva, and 2 in the plaza (Lange 1968:92).

At Pecos, trash middens and trash-filled rooms in all excavated parts of the site contained burials, and a similar situation was found at Forked Lightning (Kidder 1958). However, these two sites appear to differ from Arroyo Hondo and the rest of the comparative sites in their scarcity of subfloor burials. No subfloor pits were noted at Forked Lightning, and with regard to Pecos, Kidder (1958:280) wrote:

> although we found some few examples of a grave dug through a floor, we could almost always make out that its shaft had been sunk in an accumulation of refuse *on* the floor. And among the many Pecos interments below rooms we found no single grave-size mend in a floor to show that a burial had been put through it and the room continued in use.

Despite such intersite variation in the kinds of burial locations, Arroyo Hondo seems to fit a general pattern of interment throughout a site in plazas, trash middens, and beneath the floors or in the trash fill of rooms.

Body Position and Orientation

At Arroyo Hondo, the bodies of the dead were almost invariably placed flexed in single graves. This practice seems to have been standard at all the sites examined for comparison, although a few extended skeletons and group interments have been reported. Beyond this generalization, no particular body position was strongly predominant at Arroyo Hondo or any of the other sites. As can be seen in Table 25, each of the four main positions was fairly well represented at each site.

There was a slight trend at Arroyo Hondo for burials to be oriented toward the east, a situation also observed at Paa-ko (see Table 26). However, the general pattern throughout the northern Rio Grande region seems to have included no single typical direction of head orientation. Referring to Pecos, Kidder (1958:288) noted:

> Interments in sloping middens . . . were usually made parallel to the slope, but with no preference for one direction or the other. Many graves, particularly of infants, were sited without regard to the incline. Those in open middens on the relatively flat-surfaced

mesilla, were headed toward all points of the compass. Where a wall was involved, the grave was generally run along it, again with no directional preference.

Proximity to structures might also have influenced grave orientation at Arroyo Hondo, since most burial pits located near walls were oriented parallel to the long axis of the structure (Kepp 1972:25).

TABLE 25.
Body positions of burials at sites in the northern Rio Grande region. (Numbers refer to number of individuals. No data available from the Alfred Herrera site.)

	Left Side	Right Side	On Face	On Back	Sitting	Unknown	Total
FORKED LIGHTNING							
Number	30	21	13	47		41	152
Percent	19.7	13.8	8.6	30.9		27.0	
PINDI							
Number	7	11	14	9	2	43	86
Percent	8.1	12.8	16.3	10.5	2.3	50.0	
PAA-KO							
Number	36	35	18	36	1	20	146
Percent	24.7	23.9	12.3	24.7	0.7	13.7	
PECOS (Black-on-white Period)							
Number	9	10	12	18			49
Percent	18.4	20.4	24.5	36.7			
PECOS (Glaze I Period)							
Number	27	31	38	11			107
Percent	25.2	29.0	35.5	10.3			
ARROYO HONDO							
Number	25	27	13	17		29	111
Percent	22.5	24.3	11.7	15.3		26.1	

Grave Accoutrements

Mortuary offerings were frequently buried with the dead at Arroyo Hondo, especially if the deceased was under the age of about 15. Seventy of the excavated burials (63 percent) contained grave goods of

TABLE 26.
Head orientations of burials at northern Rio Grande sites. (Numbers refer to number of individuals. No data available from Pecos.)

	N	S	E	W	NW	NE	SW	SE	Zenith	Unknown	Total
FORKED LIGHTNING											
Adults	17	12	7	17							53
Immatures	6	12	4	21							43
Total	23	24	11	38							96
Percent	24.0	25.0	11.4	39.6							
PINDI											
Number	13	15	20	14	2			2	2	18	86
Percent	15.1	17.4	23.3	16.3	2.3			2.3	2.3	20.9	
PAA-KO											
Number	24	14	60	15	5	5	2	4	1	16	146
Percent	16.4	9.6	41.1	10.3	3.4	3.4	1.4	2.7	0.7	11.0	
ALFRED HERRERA											
Number	4	11	8	12	3	1	4	1		10	54
Percent	7.4	20.4	14.8	22.2	5.6	1.8	7.4	1.8		18.6	
ARROYO HONDO											
Number	17	19	41	14						20	111
Percent	15.3	17.1	36.9	12.6						18.0	

some sort, with 45 percent of the adults and 75 percent of the subadults contributing to this total. It was common practice to wrap the body in a hide blanket and to place it in the grave on a mat woven of yucca fiber. These blankets and mats appeared most often with subadults, of whom 54 percent had one or both items, but were also found with 27 percent of the adult burials. Food offerings, particularly ears of corn, were sometimes placed with the body, as were personal items such as shell and stone jewelry, pottery, and stone and wood tools. Few of the grave accoutrements could be called elaborate, however, and most burials included only one or two items.

The incidence of grave goods with individuals of different ages suggested that children under six were given mortuary treatment different from that received by older people. Those below six years of age were significantly more often buried with hide blankets or yucca mats, while adults were significantly more often accompanied by rare or unusual items. Two adults exhibited traces of body paint, and a third was buried with a collection of items interpreted as ceremonial equipment. These observations supported the hypothesis that the Arroyo Hondo inhabitants, like the present-day Tewas, practiced a system of age and status grading in which children under six and adults with ceremonial positions were distinguished from the other, ordinary members of society.

The kinds of grave accoutrements seen at Arroyo Hondo appear to be typical of those found throughout the northern Rio Grande during the fourteenth century. At Forked Lightning, individuals were "apparently always wrapped in twilled rush matting" (Kidder 1958:28). Stubbs and Stallings (1953:145) felt that at Pindi, the use of grass matting "to cover or wrap the body" was a "general custom." The remains of "rotten matting" were found with seven individuals at Paa-ko (Lambert 1954:167), and mats, hides, feather robes, and textiles were recovered with burials at Pecos (Kidder 1958). A list of other types of mortuary artifacts at these sites would include pottery; shell, bone, and stone ornaments; turquoise; foodstuff; clay pipes; and stone tools such as metates and axes. Although no two sites are exactly alike in terms of grave goods, the overall inventory corresponds well with that from Arroyo Hondo.

Grave accoutrements seem to have been somewhat commoner at Arroyo Hondo Pueblo than at most of the other sites reviewed in this study. With 63 percent of all individuals accompanied by mortuary

71

items, Arroyo Hondo is followed closely by the Alfred Herrera site, where "burial offerings were present in perhaps half of the cases" (Lange 1968:92). At the other sites, grave goods occurred with only about 17 percent to 34 percent of all individuals. However, it is uncertain whether this difference is real or only apparent, since the statistics might be affected by varying excavation methods, recording, or reporting. In any case, it seems clear that grave accoutrements were not indispensable to mortuary rites in the northern Rio Grande region.

Data on the incidence of grave goods by age class are not available for most of the comparative sites, but Pindi Pueblo resembles Arroyo Hondo in that children and infants were more often accompanied by mortuary items than were adults. Stubbs and Stallings (1953:145) also note that "The few decorated objects found in burials were with infants or children." At Pecos, all shells and turquoise found in burials were associated with individuals under two years of age (Kidder 1958:295). Forked Lightning, on the other hand, differed in producing grave goods more often with adults than with children. Thus, it might be tentatively concluded that no single pattern of mortuary treatment by age class prevailed throughout the region as a whole.

SUMMARY AND COMPARISON OF SKELETAL DATA

The age distribution of the Arroyo Hondo burials showed a high infant-child mortality of 26 percent for those one year or less and 45 percent for those five years old or less. These figures correspond fairly well with the mortality rate calculated by Weiss (1973) in his model life tables for prehistoric societies. Nutrition-related pathologies were common among infants and children, and it appears that high sub-adult mortality is attributable to a synergy between malnutrition and infectious disease. Mortality among adults over 30 was much greater than that predicted by Weiss's tables, probably because of a high incidence of accidental deaths in those age classes.

Although different age categories were used in reporting data from other sites in the northern Rio Grande, the information in Table 27 indicates that Arroyo Hondo is not unusual in its high infant mortality. In the categories "infant" and "0–3 years," mortality at Forked Lightning, Pindi, Paa-ko, and Pecos ranged from 21 percent to 35 percent. It should be noted that the data from Pecos may be skewed by the

TABLE 27.
Age distribution of burials at northern Rio Grande sites.

FORKED LIGHTNING

	Age (years)							
	0–3	4–9	10–19	20–34	35–54	55+	Unknown	Total
Number	43	16	6	25	41	14	7	152
Percent	28.3	10.5	3.9	16.5	27.0	9.2	4.6	

PINDI

	Infant	Child	Adult	Total
Number	29	11	46	86
Percent	33.7	12.8	53.5	

PAA-KO

	Infant	Child	Youth	Adult	Total
Number	51	28	9	58	146
Percent	34.9	19.2	6.2	39.7	

PECOS
Black-on-white Period

	Age (years)								
	0–1	1–3	3–9	10–20	20–30	30–50	50+	Unknown	Total
Number	12	8	5	6	8	15	7	1	62
Percent	19.3	12.9	8.1	9.7	12.9	24.2	11.3	1.6	

Glaze I Period

	0–1	1–3	3–9	10–20	20–30	30–50	50+	Unknown	Total
Number	12	7	7	12	20	37	24	5	124
Percent	9.8	5.6	5.6	9.8	16.1	29.8	19.3	4.0	

ALFRED HERRERA SITE

	Age (years)								
	0–3	4–8	9–12	13–17	18–20	21–35	36–55	56+	Total
Number	6	4	0	1	1	18	19	5	54
Percent	11.1	7.4	0	1.8	1.8	33.4	35.2	9.3	

counting only of individuals accompanied by pottery. The Alfred Herrera site seems to diverge from the general pattern, with 11 percent of its burials in the 0–3 group and almost 67 percent in the 21–55 categories.

The adult sex ratio at Arroyo Hondo was normal in that statistically the burials could have been drawn from a population 50 percent female and 50 percent male. Comparative data are available from three sites. Forked Lightning burials included 42 adult males and 39 adult females, which again seems to be a biologically acceptable distribution. At Pecos, Hooton (1930:32) reported 72 adult males and 52 adult females in a partial sample of the Black-on-white and Glaze I period burials. A ratio of 30 adult males to 12 adult females was noted at the Alfred Herrera site (Heglar in Lange 1968:269). No ready explanation for the seemingly high male-female ratio at the Alfred Herrera site can be offered.

In stature, the Arroyo Hondo adult males averaged 163.87 cm, the females 156.24 cm. Compared with stature reconstructions from three other sites (Table 28), the mean for the Arroyo Hondo females was similar to the mean female height at the Alfred Herrera site and slightly greater than that at Paa-ko and Pecos. Adult males at Arroyo Hondo seem to be comparable to those at Pecos and the Alfred Herrera site and about 5 cm taller, on the average, than those at Paa-ko.

TABLE 28.
Stature reconstructions for burial samples from the northern Rio Grande region.

	Number of Specimens	Range (cm)	Mean (cm)	Standard Deviation	Variance
PAA-KO[1]					
Male	19	152–168	158.74±1.39	5.29±0.58	3.33±0.54
Female	5	148–159	151.85±1.89	4.24±0.91	2.79±0.60
PECOS[2]					
Male	22	154–176	161.86±0.70	4.85±0.49	3.00±0.30
Female	17	147–158	152.00±0.46	2.79±0.32	1.84±0.21
ALFRED HERRERA SITE[3]					
Male	25	155–175	164.80		
Female	11	149–163	155.27		

[1]Reported by Rogers (1954:27), who used the Pearson formula for stature reconstruction.
[2]Reported by Hooten (1930:178), who also used the Pearson formula.
[3]Reported by Heglar in Lange (1968:269), using Telkka (1950).

Nearly half (44 percent) of all individuals in the Arroyo Hondo skeletal population exhibited bone pathologies. Predominant among those were bowing of the long bones, porotic hyperostosis, porosity, endocranial lesions, cribra orbitalia, and periostitis, all associated with nutritional or disease stresses. Because the analysis of skeletal pathologies at Arroyo Hondo focused on these nutrition- and disease-related conditions rather than on pathologies caused by trauma or aging, the data are not directly comparable with those from other sites. However, "cranial exotoses" were noted at Paa-ko (Rogers 1954:26), and two cases of cranial vault periostitis with thickening of the cranial diploe were reported at the Alfred Herrera site (Heglar in Lange 1968:266). Pathologies observed in the Black-on-white and Glaze I period skeletons at Pecos (Hooton 1930:320– 30) included periostitis, osteomyelitis, and "osteoporosis symmetrica," currently known as porotic or spongy hyperostosis. The most common kinds of skeletal pathologies reported in the northern Rio Grande region are osteoarthritis, traumatic injuries, and dental disease.

CONCLUSIONS

A review of northern Rio Grande sites contemporaneous with Arroyo Hondo Pueblo did not reveal any single set of mortuary practices consistent throughout the region. Still, Arroyo Hondo seems generally similar to other sites in its pattern of flexed burials in separate pits found in rooms, plazas, and trash middens; in its lack of a standard body position or orientation; and in the practice of burying some individuals with grave goods such as hide blankets, yucca mats, pottery, and shell and stone jewelry. The pueblo's high infant-child mortality also seems typical of the region. Genetically, the Arroyo Hondo population appears most similar to other prehistoric skeletal series of probable Tewa-Tano affiliation (see Mackey, Appendix G). This finding, based on a multivariate analysis of discrete cranial traits, is consistent with other biological distance studies of prehistoric Pueblo populations (Corruccini 1972; Heglar 1974: Lumpkin 1976; Mackey 1977).

The Arroyo Hondo skeletal sample was large enough to allow the testing of some propositions about the demography and social organization of the Component I community. Because nutrition-related pathologies were prevalent among the subadults, it is felt that dietary stress was a major cause of the high infant-child mortality observed in life tables constructed for the pueblo. Socially, the Arroyo Hondo inhabitants seem to have shared certain elements of present-day Tewa organization, in that three main status distinctions based on age and position in the ceremonial hierarchy are reflected in the mortuary remains.

Appendix A

SUMMARY OF SKELETAL MATERIAL
EXCAVATED BY NELSON (1915)

BURIAL 1

Age: Adult. Sex: No data. Condition: Head and bones of the lower legs missing. Location: In fill of room 12-1-1, northwest corner. Orientation: East-west, based on drawing. Associated Materials: A large culinary jar was found set upon some stones and resting against the knee. The vessel was broken but appeared to be complete. Its mouth was oriented up.

BURIAL 2

Age: Adult. Sex: No data. Condition: Complete. Location: In fill of room 12-1-3, about one foot above the floor, in northeast corner according to sketch but in southwest corner according to notes. Orientation: Head to the north, face turned to the west. Associated Materials: A "whitish chert" projectile point (catalogue no. 621 A) was "found between the heels and buttocks of the skeleton." Burial was photographed.

BURIAL 3

Age: Infant. Sex: Immature. Condition: Fragmentary and incomplete. Location: "Slightly" below floor in room 12-2-22, southeast corner. Orientation: No data. Associated Materials: No data.

BURIAL 4

Age: Adult. *Sex:* Female(?) *Condition:* Fragmentary and incomplete. *Location:* Just under upper floor of room 12-16-1, southeast corner. *Orientation:* No data. *Associated Materials:* Infant skeleton, Burial 5. *Comments:* This room is located on the north side of roomblock 16 and was involved in the room collapse in that area. Accidental death.

BURIAL 5

Age: Infant. *Sex:* Immature. *Condition:* No data. *Location:* Just under upper floor of room 12-16-1, southeast corner. *Orientation:* No data. *Associated Materials:* Adult skeleton, Burial 4. *Comments:* See Burial 4; accidental death.

BURIAL 6

Age: Adult. *Sex:* Female(?) *Condition:* Fragmentary and incomplete. *Location:* On floor of room 12-16-1, southwest corner. *Orientation:* No data. *Associated Material:* Child skeleton, Burial 7. *Comments:* See Burial 4; accidental death.

BURIAL 7

Age: Child. *Sex:* Immature. *Condition:* No data. *Location:* On floor of room 12-16-1, southwest corner. *Orientation:* No data. *Associated Materials:* Adult skeleton, Burial 6. *Comments:* See Burial 4; accidental death.

BURIAL 8

Age: Adult. *Sex:* No data. *Condition:* Fragmentary and incomplete. *Location:* On floor of room 12-19-2, "across south end of room." *Orientation:* No data. *Associated Materials:* No data. *Comments:* Accidental death.

BURIAL 9

Age: Infant. *Sex:* Immature. *Condition:* Fragmentary and incomplete. *Location:* In fill of room 12-20-2. *Orientation:* No data. *Associated Materials:* No data.

BURIAL 10

Age: Adult. *Sex:* No data. *Condition:* Fragmentary and incomplete. *Location:* In fill of room 12-23-3. *Associated Materials:* No data.

BURIAL 11

Age: Infant. *Sex:* Immature. *Condition:* Fragmentary. *Location:* Trench on south side of roomblock 24. *Orientation:* No data. *Associated Materials:* No data. *Comments:* Nelson notes that "several informants state that a number of skeletons have been washed out in the adjoining gulch."

MISCELLANEOUS INFORMATION

Ash Heap A: "Deposit a more or less visibly stratified mixture of ashes and charcoal, a very few animal bones, fragments of stone implements, pot sherds and human burials. . . . Items Found: 1) Adult female skeleton, fragmentary and incomplete (taken)" (Burial 12).

Refuse Heap C: "Items Found: 1) Traces of skeletons."

In his field notes, Nelson (1915:5) mentions that "Over 30 skeletons, representing all ages were exhumed. With one, a child of 5–6 was found traces of a necklace of shell and turquoise, as well as pendants."

ISOLATED REMAINS FROM THE FILL OF
ROOMS REEXCAVATED BY S.A.R.

Room 12-1-5: Fragments of infant skull.

Room 12-11-4: Pelvis bone, fragmentary.

Room 12-18-2: Humerus and fragments of tibia of adult.

Room 12-20-2: Adult human jaw bone, fragmentary.

Room 12-16-1: Right half of adult mandible with second premolar and first and second molars; left scapula; occipital fragment; left petrous fragment; long bone fragments; and miscellaneous fragments.

Appendix B

LOCATIONS OF BURIALS AT
ARROYO HONDO PUEBLO

The locations of all formal burials and accidental deaths recovered at Arroyo Hondo Pueblo are shown on the following series of site plans. Because of its large size, the entire pueblo could not be drawn as a single figure at a scale large enough to show any detail. Therefore, the site was divided into groups of roomblocks and plazas small enough to be shown at a reasonable scale on one page. These portions of the site, Figures 22 through 27, are keyed to two schematic plans of the entire pueblo—one plan for Component I (Fig. 20) and one for Component II (Fig. 21). By referring back to these overall site maps, the reader can place the burial locations within the larger context of the pueblo. Only the portions of the site in which burials were found are shown here.

On the smaller plans, features are distinguished according to the following scheme:

▬▬▬	excavated adobe room
▬▬▬	unexcavated adobe room
▬ ▬ ▬	probable adobe wall
◻◻◻◻◻	excavated masonry room

• • • • • • • • • • • unexcavated masonry room

▬▬ • ▬▬ limits of excavation in plazas, test trenches, test pits, and so forth.

Number designations refer to roomblocks, letter designations to plazas. A combination of a letter and a number (for example, G-5) refers to a kiva.

Each burial is shown by a symbol according to the following key:

 subadult, known orientation

 subadult, unknown orientation

 adult female, known orientation

 adult male, known orientation

 adult, known orientation, unknown sex

 adult, unknown orientation.

Where orientation is known, the circle indicates the direction of the head.

Each burial symbol is accompanied by a number that is keyed to a list of specimen numbers following the plan drawings. For example, the list shows that Burial 15 in Figure 23 is specimen number 12-K-3-IV (I). A second list then presents all burials by number according to their spatial proveniences; for example, all those in plaza C or all those found in rooms. Full descriptions of all individuals can be found in Appendix D.

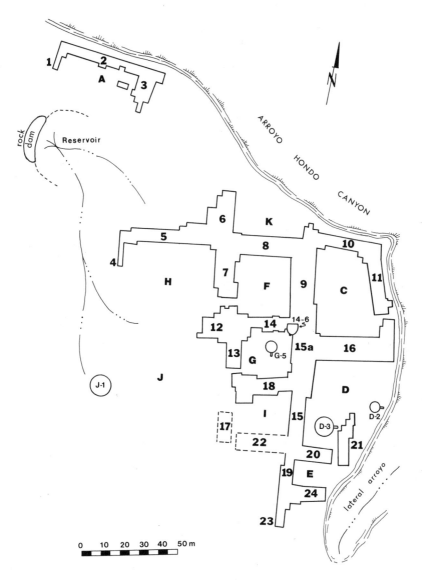

FIG. 20. Schematic plan of Arroyo Hondo Pueblo, Component I.

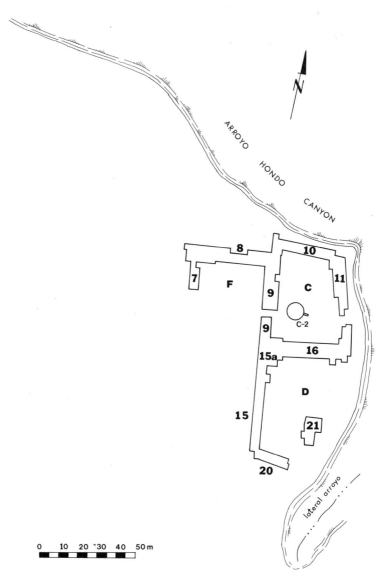

FIG. 21.   Schematic plan of Arroyo Hondo Pueblo, Component II.

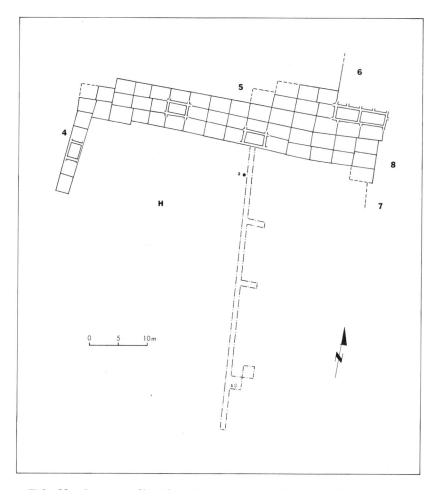

FIG. 22.   Locations of burials in Component I plaza H and roomblocks 4 and 5.

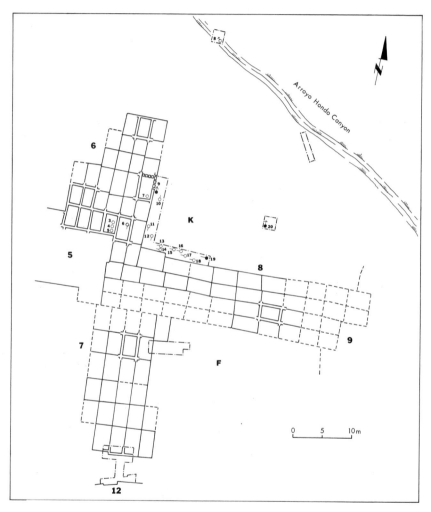

FIG. 23.   Locations of burials in Component I plazas F and K and roomblocks 6, 7, and 8.

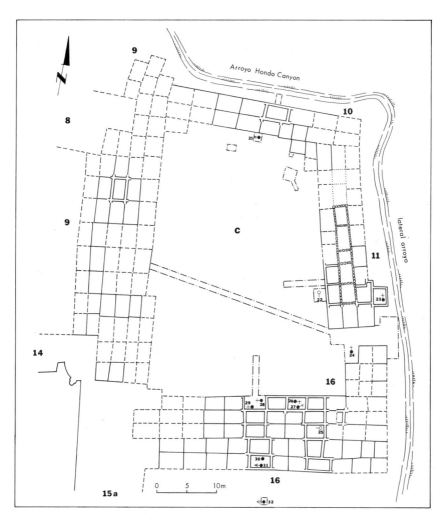

FIG. 24. Locations of burials in Component I plaza C and roomblocks 9, 10, 11, and 16.

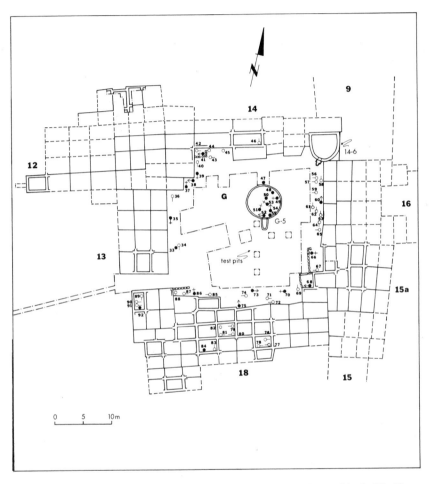

FIG. 25.   Locations of burials in Component I plaza G and roomblocks 12, 13, 14, 15A, and 18.

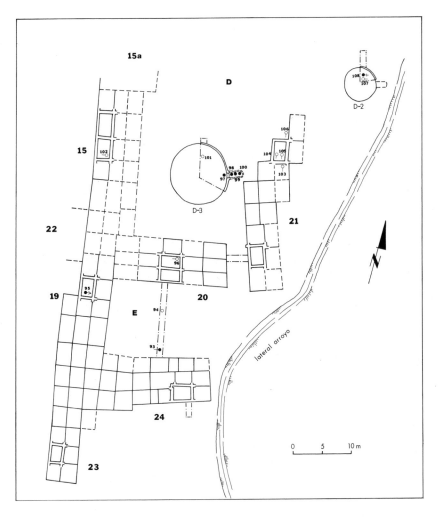

FIG. 26.   Locations of burials in Component I plazas D and E and roomblocks 15, 19, 20, 21, 23, and 24.

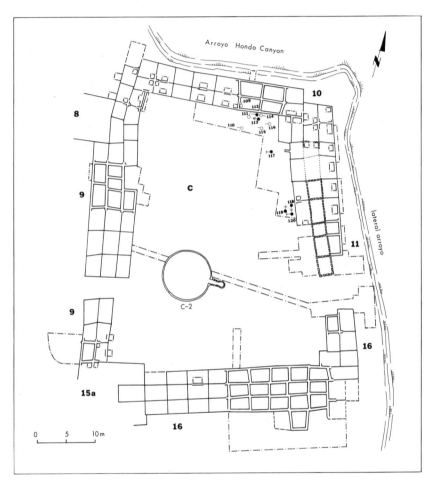

FIG. 27.   Locations of burials in Component II plaza C and roomblocks 9, 10, 11, and 16.

LIST OF BURIAL NUMBERS CORRESPONDING TO SITE PLANS

1. 12-H-1-0-1 (Fig. 22)
2. 12-H-3-7-3 (Fig. 22)
3. 12-6-8-6E-3 (A) (Fig. 23)
4. 12-6-8-6E-3 (B) (Fig. 23)
5. 12-6-8-6E-3 (C) (Fig. 23)
6. 12-6-14-5-1 (Fig. 23)
7. 12-6-6-5 (Fig. 23)
8. 12-K-1 (Fig. 23)
9. 12-K-16-IV-1 (H) (Fig. 23)
10. 12-K-15-IV (G) (Fig. 23)
11. 12-K-12-IV (F) (Fig. 23)
12. 12-K-12-IV (E) (Fig. 23)
13. 12-K-3-III (A1) (Fig. 23)
14. 12-K-3-III (A2) (Fig. 23)
15. 12-K-3-IV (I) (Fig. 23)
16. 12-K-3-IV (J) (Fig. 23)
17. 12-K-4-III (B) (Fig. 23)
18. 12-K-4-III (C) (Fig. 23)
19. 12-K-6-II (D) (Fig. 23)
20. 12-K-SQ3-3-7 (Fig. 23)
21. 12-C-A-12-1 (Fig. 24)
22. 12-11-3A-2-2 (Fig. 24)
23. 12-11-8-2-1-3 (Fig. 24)
24. 12-16-38-6 (Fig. 24)
25. 12-16-31-11-1 (Fig. 24)
26. 12-16-37-3 (Fig. 24)
27. 12-16-37-4 (Fig. 24)
28. 12-16-29-5-1 (Fig. 24)
29. 12-16-29-2-9 (Fig. 24)
30. 12-16-36-5-2 (Fig. 24)
31. 12-16-36-4-1 (Fig. 24)
32. 12-D-1-7 (Fig. 24)
33. 12-G-1C-2-2 (Fig. 25)
34. 12-G-1C-3-1 (Fig. 25)
35. 12-G-2-3-14 (Fig. 25)
36. 12-G-2-3-84 (Fig. 25)
37. 12-G-2-4-36 (Fig. 25)
38. 12-G-2-4-34 (Fig. 25)
39. 12-G-4-61 (Fig. 25)
40. 12-G-2-4-47 (Fig. 25)
41. 12-G-2-4-14 (Fig. 25)
42. 12-G-2-4-12 (Fig. 25)
43. 12-G-2-4-63 (Fig. 25)
44. 12-G-2-4-10 (Fig. 25)
45. 12-G-2-4-8 (Fig. 25)
46. 12-14-5-8-1 (Fig. 25)
47. 12-G-6 (Fig. 25)
48. 12-G-5-6 (Fig. 25)
49. 12-G-5-2 (Fig. 25)
50. 12-G-5-8 (Fig. 25)
51. 12-G-5-5 (Fig. 25)
52. 12-G-5-7 (Fig. 25)
53. 12-G-5-4 (Fig. 25)
54. 12-G-5-3 (Fig. 25)
55. 12-G-5-1 (Fig. 25)
56. 12-G-D8-4-1 (Fig. 25)
57. 12-G-D8-4-2 (Fig. 25)
58. 12-G-D8-4-3 (Fig. 25)
59. 12-G-D6-4-1 (Fig. 25)
60. 12-G-D4-4-1 (Fig. 25)
61. 12-G-D2-4-2 (Fig. 25)
62. 12-G-D2-4-1 (Fig. 25)
63. 12-G-2-3-159 (Fig. 25)
64. 12-G-ST7-2-10 (Fig. 25)
65. 12-G-ST7-3-2 (Fig. 25)
66. 12-G-2-3-35 (Fig. 25)
67. 12-G-2-3-198 (Fig. 25)
68. 12-G-2-3-28 (Fig. 25)
69. 12-G-2-3-27 (Fig. 25)
70. 12-G-2-3-29 (Fig. 25)
71. 12-G-B110-2 (Fig. 25)
72. 12-G-B110-3 (Fig. 25)
73. 12-G-B111-4 (Fig. 25)
74. 12-G-B110-4 (Fig. 25)
75. 12-G-2-3-22 (Fig. 25)
76. 12-18-6-3S-2 (Fig. 25)
77. 12-18-6-3S-8 (Fig. 25)
78. 12-18-6-3S-15 (Fig. 25)
79. 12-18-8-4N-9 (Fig. 25)
80. 12-18-8-4S-8 (Fig. 25)
81. 12-18-8-VI-1 (Fig. 25)
82. 12-18-8-VII-1 (Fig. 25)
83. 12-18-39-IV-9 (Fig. 25)
84. 12-18-39-IS-1 (Fig. 25)
85. 12-G-30A-2A-1 (Fig. 25)
86. 12-G-2-3-37 (Fig. 25)
87. 12-G-2-3-21-2 (Fig. 25)
88. 12-G-2-3-21-1 (Fig. 25)
89. 12-18-15-IN-1 (Fig. 25)
90. 12-18-15-IN-2 (Fig. 25)
91. 12-18-15-IN-3 (Fig. 25)
92. 12-18-15-IN-4 (Fig. 25)
93. 12-E-1-1 (Fig. 26)
94. 12-E-1-2 (Fig. 26)
95. 12-19-1-V-1 (Fig. 26)
96. 12-20-6-5-1 (Fig. 26)

97. 12-D-3-1-2 (Fig. 26)
98. 12-D-3-1-3 (Fig. 26)
99. 12-D-3-1-4 (Fig. 26)
100. 12-D-3-1-5 (Fig. 26)
101. 12-D-3-1-1 (Fig. 26)
102. 12-15-7-5-1 (Fig. 26)
103. 12-21-4-1-5 (Fig. 26)
104. 12-21-3-12-2 (Fig. 26)
105. 12-21-3-III-1 (Fig. 26)
106. 12-21-5-1-3 (Fig. 26)
107. 12-D-2-2-2 (Fig. 26)
108. 12-D-2-2-1 (Fig. 26)

109. 12-10-4-6 (Fig. 27)
110. 12-C-9-1-1 (Fig. 27)
111. 12-C-A-8-1 (Fig. 27)
112. 12-C-A-7-1 (Fig. 27)
113. 12-C-A-4-2 (Fig. 27)
114. 12-C-A-4-3 (Fig. 27)
115. 12-C-A-6-1-1 (Fig. 27)
116. 12-C-A-2-1 (Fig. 27)
117. 12-C-A-20-1-2 (Fig. 27)
118. 12-C-A-39-1 (Fig. 27)
119. 12-C-A-39-2 (Fig. 27)
120. 12-C-A-39-3-3 (Fig. 27)

LIST OF BURIALS BY LOCATION (Burial numbers from preceding list and Figures 22–27).

COMPONENT I

PLAZA C
Subadult:
22. 12-11-3A-2-2
Adult:
21. 12-C-A-12-1
29. 12-16-29-2-9
28. 12-16-29-5-1

PLAZA D
Subadult:
106. 12-21-5-1-3

PLAZA G
Primary Plaza Surface 3
Subadult:
59. 12-G-D6-4-1
58. 12-G-D8-4-3
65. 12-G-ST7-3-2
67. 12-G-2-3-198
43. 12-G-2-4-63
46. 12-14-5-8-1
Adult:
73. 12-G-B111-4

Primary Plaza Surface 2
Subadult:
71. 12-G-B110-2
72. 12-G-B110-3
74. 12-G-B110-4
62. 12-G-D2-4-1
61. 12-G-D2-4-2
56. 12-G-D8-4-1
57. 12-G-D8-4-2
64. 12-G-ST7-2-10

42. 12-G-2-4-12
40. 12-G-2-4-47
Adult:
60. 12-G-D4-4-1
68. 12-G-2-3-28
41. 12-G-2-4-14

Primary Plaza Surface 1
Subadult:
34. 12-G-1C-3-1
88. 12-G-2-3-21-1
87. 12-G-2-3-21-2
36. 12-G-2-3-84
63. 12-G-2-3-159
85. 12-G-30A-2A-1
Adult:
35. 12-G-2-3-14
75. 12-G-2-3-22
70. 12-G-2-3-29
66. 12-G-2-3-35
38. 12-G-2-4-34
37. 12-G-2-4-36
39. 12-G-4-61

Trash Postdating Surface 1
Subadult:
69. 12-G-2-3-27
45. 12-G-2-4-8
44. 12-G-2-4-10
Adult:
33. 12-G-1C-2-2
86. 12-G-2-3-37

PLAZA K
Subadult:
13. 12-K-3-III Pit A (1)
14. 12-K-3-III Pit A (2)
17. 12-K-4-III Pit B
18. 12-K-4-III Pit C
12. 12-K-12-IV Pit E
11. 12-K-12-IV Pit F
10. 12-K-15-IV Pit G
15. 12-K-3-IV Pit I
16. 12-K-3-IV Pit J
Adult:
9. 12-K-16-IV-1 Pit H

*TRASH MIDDENS
IN PLAZAS*
Subadult:
107. 12-D-2-2-2
101. 12-D-3-1-1
94. 12-E-1-2
2. 12-H-3-7-3
8. 12-K-1
Adult:
32. 12-D-1-7
108. 12-D-2-2-1
97. 12-D-3-1-2
98. 12-D-3-1-3
99. 12-D-3-1-4
100. 12-D-3-1-5
93. 12-E-1-1
55. 12-G-5-1
47. 12-G-6
1. 12-H-1-0-1
20. 12-K-SQ3-3-7
19. 12-K-6-II Pit D
24. 12-16-38-6

ROOMS
Subfloor Pits
Subadult:
7. 12-6-6-5
6. 12-6-14-5-1
102. 12-15-7-5-1
25. 12-16-31-11-1
76. 12-18-6-3S-2
77. 12-18-6-3S-8
78. 12-18-6-3S-15
80. 12-18-8-4S-8
79. 12-18-8-4N-9
82. 12-18-8-VII-1
83. 12-18-39-IV-9

96. 12-20-6-5-1
105. 12-21-3-III-1
104. 12-21-3-12-2
103. 12-21-4-1-5
Adult:
23. 12-11-8-2-1-3
31. 12-16-36-4-1
30. 12-16-36-5-2
81. 12-18-8-VI-1
95. 12-19-1-V-1

Roof Fall
Subadult:
3. 12-6-8-6E-3A
4. 12-6-8-6E-3B
5. 12-6-8-6E-3C

Trash Fill in Rooms
Subadult:
89. 12-18-15-IN-1
90. 12-18-15-IN-2
91. 12-18-15-IN-3
Adult:
84. 12-18-39-IS-1
92. 12-18-15-IN-4

ACCIDENTAL DEATHS
Adult:
49. 12-G-5-2
54. 12-G-5-3
53. 12-G-5-4
51. 12-G-5-5
48. 12-G-5-6
52. 12-G-5-7
50. 12-G-5-8
26. 12-16-37-3
27. 12-16-37-4

COMPONENT II

PLAZA C
Plaza Surface 1
Adult:
113. 12-C-A-4-2
118. 12-C-A-39-1
119. 12-C-A-39-2
120. 12-C-A-39-3-3

Plaza Surface 2
Subadult:
116. 12-C-A-2-1
114. 12-C-A-4-3
111. 12-C-A-8-1

Plaza Surface 4
Adult:
  112. 12-C-A-7-1

TRASH MIDDENS
  IN PLAZAS
Subadult:
  115. 12-C-A-6-1-1

110. 12-C-9-1-1
Adult:
  117. 12-C-A-20-1-2

ROOMS
Subadult:
  109. 12-10-4-6

Appendix C

SKELETAL AGE AND SEX CRITERIA, SKELETAL MEASUREMENTS, AND STATURE ESTIMATES

AGE AND SEX CRITERIA

The age standards employed in this study, roughly in order of reliability, were as follows:

1. Dental development and eruption (Kronfeld 1935; Schour and Massler 1941; Moorrees, Fanning, and Hunt 1963a, 1963b; Anderson, Thompson, and Popovich 1976)
2. Skeletal growth and development (occipital development: Redfield 1970; vertebral development: Breathnach 1965, Goss 1966; metopic suture closure: Krogman 1963; long bone growth: Johnston 1962, Ubelaker 1978)
3. Epiphyseal union (Stevenson 1924; Todd and D'Errico 1928; Francis and Werle 1939; Flecker 1942; McKern and Stewart 1957; Modi 1957; Vallois 1960; Johnston 1961; Mackay 1961; Krogman 1962; McKern 1970)

4. Pubic symphysis changes (Todd 1920, 1921, 1923; McKern and Stewart 1957; Kerley 1970; Gilbert and McKern 1971)
5. Endocranial suture closure (Todd and Lyon 1924, 1925; Krogman 1962; Kerley 1970).

The various age criteria were applied to the age groups for which they were appropriate. In the subadult class, ages were determined by dental development, using calcification standards suggested by Ubelaker (1974). Eruption standards normally employed in skeletal studies were used to cross-check these age determinations. When teeth were absent, skeletal growth and development substituted as age criteria. These criteria included occipital developmental changes and size comparisons with individuals in the Arroyo Hondo skeletal series whose ages had been estimated through other means. Laboratory specimens of known age were also used as cross-references for determining age by skeletal development.

The ages of young adults were estimated using epiphyseal union standards. For adults up to about 50 years old, separate male and female standards of pubic symphysis changes were employed. Endocranial suture closure was utilized as a standard of last resort when other age criteria for adults could not be applied. Adult age estimates were cross-checked according to osteophytosis development (Stewart 1958; Kerley 1970) and intrapopulation dental wear, both of which served to corroborate the general age range to which an individual had been assigned. Because of the variable bone preservation at Arroyo Hondo, aging criteria based on internal bone remodeling could not be used (Palkovich 1978). Since other means of aging older adult skeletons are largely unreliable, age was not estimated for those over 50 years, and instead they were lumped in a 50+ category.

Criteria used for adult sex determination were those presented by Acsádi and Nemeskéri (1970), Dwight (1904–5), Krogman (1962), Maltby (1917–18), Parsons (1914–15), Pearson (1917–19), Phenice (1969), Thieme and Schull (1957), and Washburn (1948). Methods for determining the sex of subadults are usually based on differences in the relationships between soft tissue and skeletal parts or on differential growth rates. These methods require further refinement to increase their reliability when applied to skeletal remains. Therefore, sex was not determined for subadults in this study, and no assumptions were made about the distribution of males and females in subadult age classes.

SKELETAL MEASUREMENTS AND
STATURE ESTIMATES

Standards of skeletal measurement derived from Vallois (1965) were used in order to maintain consistency with Mackey's study of the Arroyo Hondo crania (Appendix G). Stature estimates were based on Genovés (1967), when possible using the formulas he provides and otherwise deriving stature estimates from his tables. For adults whose sex could not be determined, stature was calculated as the average between male and female estimates. Because Genovés's research was based on recent indigenous populations in Mexico, his study offers the best existing criteria for estimating adult stature among prehistoric southwestern populations.

TABLE 29.
Long bone measurements: legs (cm).

Specimen Number	Sex	Right Femur	Left Femur	Right Tibia	Left Tibia	Right Fibula	Left Fibula
COMPONENT I							
12-D-1-7	M	--	--	38.0	38.1	36.6	--
12-G-B111-4	M	--	40.0	34.0	33.0	32.0	32.0
12-G-D4-4-1	M	--	--	36.2	36.0	--	--
12-G-1C-2-2	?	--	--	--	29.7	--	--
12-G-2-3-21-1	?	--	--	--	28.0	--	--
12-G-2-3-22	M	42.3	--	--	--	--	--
12-G-2-3-28	M	--	42.8	--	35.5	--	--
12-G-2-3-29	F	--	--	36.2	--	--	--
12-G-5-1	F	39.2	--	--	--	--	--
12-G-5-2	F	41.3	41.4	--	--	32.6	--
12-G-5-3	M	42.3	42.5	--	--	--	34.9
12-G-5-5	F	41.7	41.7	--	33.6	32.7	32.7
12-G-5-7	M	42.2	42.3	36.6	36.5	--	35.3
12-G-6	?	--	--	--	35.1	--	--
12-K-SQ3-3-7	F	38.2	38.6	32.0	31.8	30.7	30.3
12-K-16-IV-1(H)	M	42.0	43.0	37.0	37.0	36.2	36.7
12-16-36-4-1	M	46.7	46.9	40.6	40.5	39.5	--
12-16-37-3	F	39.1	39.1	--	32.4	32.9	33.0
12-16-37-4	F	40.2	40.3	33.3	33.6	32.7	33.1
12-16-38-6	F	43.0	43.3	--	--	--	--
12-19-1-V-1	M	--	--	--	39.3	--	--
COMPONENT II							
12-C-A-4-2	M	--	44.2	35.6	37.2	35.5	--
12-C-A-20-1-2	F	39.9	40.0	33.6	--	--	--
12-C-A-39-1	F	38.2	40.2	33.7	34.0	33.4	--

TABLE 30.
Long bone measurements: arms (cm).

COMPONENT I

Specimen Number	Sex	Right Humerus	Left Humerus	Right Radius	Left Radius	Right Ulna	Left Ulna
12-D-1-7	M	--	--	25.4	--	27.0	--
12-D-2-1	F	--	--	23.2	23.0	24.6	--
12-D-2-2-2	?	30.4	30.2	--	--	--	--
12-G-B111-4	M	29.0	29.0	23.0	23.0	25.0	24.0
12-G-D4-4-1	M	--	--	24.3	--	--	--
12-G-2-3-14	F	--	31.1	--	--	--	--
12-G-2-3-22	M	30.2	--	--	--	--	--
12-G-5-2	F	28.5	28.1	21.4	--	23.0	23.2
12-G-5-3	M	--	31.1	--	--	--	25.6
12-G-5-7	M	30.8	31.1	--	--	--	--
12-K-SQ3-3-7	F	27.2	26.5	22.2	21.7	23.7	23.5
12-K-6-II(D)	M	30.2	--	23.3	23.3	25.1	24.9
12-K-16-IV-1(H)	M	29.0	29.0	--	23.5	--	--
12-16-29-2-9	F	--	30.2	--	22.6	--	24.4
12-16-36-4-1	M	34.3	34.4	27.0	--	28.8	--
12-16-37-3	F	29.3	28.7	--	22.2	--	24.1
12-16-37-4	F	29.7	29.3	22.4	22.5	24.5	24.4
12-16-38-6	F	--	--	--	23.5	--	24.9
12-19-1-V-1	M	--	33.0	--	--	--	--

COMPONENT II

12-C-A-4-2	M	30.8	31.3	23.8	24.2	--	--
12-C-A-20-1-2	F	--	--	23.1	--	--	24.7
12-C-A-39-1	F	28.6	28.9	21.7	22.2	24.3	23.9
12-C-A-39-2	M	32.0	--	--	--	27.6	--

TABLE 31.

Stature estimates.

COMPONENT I

Specimen Number	Sex	Height (cm)	Specimen Number	Sex	Height (cm)
12-D-1-7	M	168.23	12-G-5-3	M	161.98
12-D-2-2-1	F	157.5	12-G-5-5	F	157.75
12-D-2-2-2	?	159.5	12-G-5-7	M	161.75
12-G-B111-4	M	156.78	12-G-6	?	160.90
12-G-D4-4-1	M	164.70	12-K-SQ3-3-7	F	148.68
12-G-1C-2-2	?	148.26	12-K-6-II D	M	160.0
12-G-2-3-14	F	162.0	12-K-16-IV-1 H	M	161.30
12-G-2-3-21-1	?	144.29	12-16-29-2-9	F	156.5
12-G-2-3-22	M	161.98	12-16-36-4-1	M	171.92
12-G-2-3-28	M	163.11	12-16-37-3	F	151.01
12-G-2-3-29	F	162.25	12-16-37-4	F	153.86
12-G-5-1	F	151.27	12-16-38-6	F	161.11
12-G-5-2	F	156.71	12-19-1-V-1	M	170.78

COMPONENT II

Specimen Number	Sex	Height (cm)	Specimen Number	Sex	Height (cm)
12-C-A-4-2	M	166.27	12-C-A-39-1	F	153.86
12-C-A-20-1-2	F	153.08	12-C-A-39-2	M	165.0

STATURE SUMMARY

Component I

Male:	n=11	Range:	156.78 to 171.92 cm	
		Mean:	163.87 cm	
Female:	n=11	Range:	148.68 to 162.25 cm	
		Mean:	156.24 cm	
Sex Indeterminate:	n= 4			
Total Population:	n=26	Range:	148.68 to 171.92 cm	
		Mean:	159.00 cm	

Component II

Male:	n= 2	Mean:	165.64 cm
Female:	n= 2	Mean:	153.47 cm
Total Population:	n= 4	Mean:	159.55 cm

TABLE 32.
Selected cranial metrics (mm).

	FEMALES					MALES			
	12-16-37-3	12-G-2-3-29	12-G-5-6	12-G-5-2	12-16-37-4	12-G-5-3	12-G-D4-4-1	12-K-6-II D	12-G-5-7
alveolar point–nasion	70	--	71	72	70	67	67	70	--
bizygomatic diameter	125	--	123	131	130	141	132	144	--
basion–nasion	102	103	--	99	95	--	99	142	102
height right orbit	37	--	33	34	35	34	35	37	--
cranial breadth	170	141	139	132	155	151	140	148	153
nasal height	48	--	49	50	47	50	45	49	--
nasal breadth	26	--	25	25	26	25	21	25	--
menton–nasion	114	--	--	--	116	--	108	--	--
alveolar length	55	--	52	51	54	55	45	50	--
alveolar breadth	72	--	--	60	72	61	55	65	--
basion–bregma						--	139	134	146
basion–prosthion	97	--	--	93	98	--	86	90	--
minimum frontal diameter	111	95	92	89	93	98	87	95	105
interorbital width	28	20	20	22	25	24	22	24	--

Appendix D

SKELETAL AND MORTUARY INFORMATION BY INDIVIDUAL AND LIST OF ISOLATED HUMAN BONES

The skeletal and mortuary information about each of the individuals recovered at Arroyo Hondo is presented here in terms of the following categories:

BURIAL: Specimen number.
Component: I or II.
Age: Estimated age. *Criteria:* Criteria used in determining age.
Age category: To which of the 12 age categories used in this study the individual was assigned.
Sex: Probable sex. *Criteria:* Criteria used in determining sex.
Other skeletal information: List of body parts recovered if the skeleton was incomplete; skeletal anomalies related to development rather than to disease.
Pathologies: Bone conditions caused by disease or injury.
Location: General location of burial within the site.
Position: Position and orientation of the body in the grave.
Pit dimensions: Measurements of burial pit.
Associated artifacts: List of all grave accoutrements found with the individual.
Burial reconstruction: General description of the burial.

For each individual, the list includes only the categories for which information was available. If age or sex was undetermined, for example, or if no grave goods were found, those categories were omitted. If a skeleton was essentially complete, the category "other skeletal information" was deleted. All Component I burials are grouped together and precede the Component II burials. Within each component, individuals are arranged by specimen number in alphabetical/numerical order, with all plaza (letter) designations preceding roomblock (number) designations.

BURIAL: 12-C-A-12-1.
Component: I
Age: 16– 18 years. *Criteria:* Epiphyseal union.
Age category: 15– 19.9.
Sex: Male. *Criteria:* Head of femur.
Pathologies: Bowing of left femur, left tibia, and right radius.
Location: Plaza C.
Position: Flexed, lying on back, head to east.
Pit dimensions: Depth 36 cm below Component I plaza surface; N-S 56 cm, E-W 101 cm.
Associated artifacts: Woven yucca-fiber mat.
Burial reconstruction: A pit was dug into the surface of plaza C, and the bottom was lined with a yucca mat upon which the body was placed. The pit was then filled with trashy soil distinctly different from the trash lenses overlying the Component I surface. Thus, the burial appeared to be associated with the Component I use of plaza C.

BURIAL: 12-D-1-7.
Component: I.
Age: 17– 18 years. *Criteria:* Epiphyseal union.
Age category: 15– 19.9.
Sex: Male. *Criteria:* Pelvis, cranium.
Location: Plaza D, trash deposit.
Position: Flexed, lying on right side, head to east.
Pit dimensions: Depth 48 cm below plaza surface; N-S 58 cm, E-W 103 cm.

Burial reconstruction: A plaza surface is located 84 cm below ground surface in this area of plaza D and is covered by an ashy lense with charcoal inclusions. It appeared that the burial pit had been dug through this lense and the plaza surface. Some ash and charcoal were mixed with the pit fill. The burial slightly postdated the Component I use of plaza D.

BURIAL: 12-D-2-2-1.
Component: I.
Age: 52–59 years. *Criteria:* Pubic symphysis (Gilbert and McKern 1971).
Age category: 50+.
Sex: Female. *Criteria:* Pelvis.
Pathologies: Localized periostitis on left tibia shaft; arthritic development in vertebrae.
Location: Lying on washed adobe surface of trash fill in kiva 12-D-2.
Position: Flexed, lying on left side, head to west.
Burial reconstruction: The burial had been disturbed during backhoe excavation, making burial reconstruction impossible.

BURIAL: 12-D-2-2-2.
Component: I.
Age: 14–17 years. *Criteria:* Epiphyseal union.
Age category: 15–19.9.
Other skeletal information: Second and third cervical vertebrae fused together during development.
Location: Trash fill of kiva 12-D-2.
Position: Head to west, otherwise not determinable.
Burial reconstruction: This skeleton had been badly disarticulated prehistorically. No burial pit was observable.

BURIAL: 12-D-3-1-1.
Component: I.
Age: 5½–6 years. *Criteria:* Compared with other specimens in the collection.
Age category: 5–9.9.
Location: Trash fill of kiva 12-D-3.
Burial reconstruction: Burial was disturbed during backhoe excavation, making burial reconstruction impossible.

BURIAL: 12-D-3-1-2 (female, 16–22 years)
        12-D-3-1-3 (adult female)
        12-D-3-1-4 (adult female)
        12-D-3-1-5 (adult male)

These four individuals were identified among a number of disturbed bones found in and near the ventilator of kiva 12-D-3. It appeared that one individual, probably the young female, had originally been buried in this area and that the burial had been disturbed during construction of the ventilator. The skeletons or partially decomposed bodies of at least three other individuals then seem to have been deposited in this area before the ventilator was completed. They probably were the disturbed remains of other burials encountered during excavation of the pit for the kiva. No grave goods were found, suggesting that the bodies had been informally reburied.

BURIAL: 12-E-1-1.
Component: I.
Age: 22–23 years. *Criteria:* Epiphyseal union.
Age category: 20–24.9.
Location: Borrow pit in plaza E.
Position: Flexed, lying on back, head to east.
Pit dimensions: Depth 91 cm below top of borrow pit, N-S and E-W
    dimensions undeterminable.
Burial reconstruction: The burial pit had been dug into the sterile soil
    at the bottom of the borrow pit, which later was filled with trash.
    Backhoe operations destroyed most of the burial information.

BURIAL: 12-E-1-2.
Component: I.
Age: 13–15 years. *Criteria:* Dental development, epiphyseal union.
Age category: 10–14.9.
Location: Trash fill of borrow pit in plaza E.
Burial reconstruction: This individual was completely removed by the
    backhoe and was recovered in backfill, making burial reconstruc-
    tion impossible.

BURIAL: 12-G-B110-2.
Component: I.
Age: 4–5 years. *Criteria:* Dental development.

Age category: 1–4.9.

Other skeletal information: Upper right first and second incisors fused.

Location: Along south wall of plaza G, associated with primary plaza surface 2.

Position: Semiflexed, lying on left side, head to west.

Pit dimensions: Depth 23 cm below plaza surface, N-S 41 cm, E-W 79 cm.

Associated artifacts: Woven yucca-fiber mat, leatherlike blanket, corncob.

Burial reconstruction: A pit was dug into the plaza surface and the bottom lined with a yucca mat. The body was wrapped in a hide or leather blanket, inside which a corncob was placed near the individual's feet. Additional matting was laid over the body in the grave and covered with a stone slab in the area of the legs. The pit was then filled with trashy soil but apparently was not covered or plastered at plaza level.

BURIAL: 12-G-B110-3.

Component: I.

Age: 16–18 months. *Criteria:* Dental development.

Age category: 1–4.9.

Location: Along south wall of plaza G, associated with primary plaza surface 2.

Position: Lying on right side, head to east.

Pit dimensions: Depth 18 cm below plaza surface, N-S 30 cm, E-W 65 cm.

Associated artifacts: Woven yucca-fiber mat, leatherlike blanket.

Burial reconstruction: A pit was dug into the plaza surface and the bottom lined with a yucca mat. The body of the infant was wrapped in a hide or leather blanket and covered with additional matting in the grave. A stone slab lay over the matting in the area of the head. The pit was then filled with trashy soil but apparently was not covered or plastered at plaza level.

BURIAL: 12-G-B110-4.

Component: I.

Age: 2½–3 months. *Criteria:* Dental development.

Age category: 0–1.

Pathologies: Periostitis on internal surface of the wing of the sphenoid.

Location: Along south wall of plaza G, associated with primary plaza
surface 2.

Position: Lying on back, head to east.

Pit dimensions: Depth 25 cm below plaza surface, N-S 25 cm, E-W
40 cm.

Associated artifacts: Woven yucca-fiber mat, leatherlike blanket.

Burial reconstruction: A burial pit was dug in the plaza surface next to
the wall. The body of the infant was wrapped in a hide blanket,
placed on a yucca mat that covered the bottom of the pit, and
covered with more matting. The pit was then filled with trashy
soil and a stone slab, but it was not covered or plastered at plaza
level.

BURIAL: 12-G-B111-4.

Component: I.

Age: 25– 28 years. *Criteria:* Pubic symphysis (Todd 1923).

Age category: 25– 29.9.

Sex: Male. *Criteria:* Pelvis, cranium.

Other skeletal information: First cervical vertebra fused to occipital
condyles.

Pathologies: Small osteoma on distal shaft of left femur; bowing evident in both femurs.

Location: Along south wall of plaza G, associated with primary plaza
surface 3.

Position: Flexed, lying on left side, head to west.

Pit dimensions: Depth 107 cm below plaza surface, N-S 44 cm, E-W
115 cm.

Associated artifacts: Woven yucca-fiber mat.

Burial reconstruction: A pit was dug into the plaza surface and the
bottom lined with a yucca mat. The body was placed on the mat,
and the pit was then filled with trashy soil. No pit outline was
visible at the level of plaza surface 3, and the pit may have been
plastered or covered by a layer of compacted soil.

BURIAL: 12-G-D2-4-1.

Component: I.

Age: 1– 1½ months. *Criteria:* Dental development.

Age category: 0– 1.

Pathologies: Cribra orbitalia; narrowing of midshafts of femurs; bowing evident in femurs and humeri; porosity evident at ends of long bones.

Location: Trash deposit above primary plaza surface 3 near east wall of plaza G.

Position: Flexed, lying on back, head to south.

Pit dimensions: Depth 13 cm below plaza surface 2, N-S 36 cm, E-W 19 cm.

Associated artifacts: Leatherlike blanket.

Burial reconstruction: Sometime before the formation of primary plaza surface 2, a pit was dug into the thin trash deposits overlying plaza surface 3. The infant's body was wrapped in a hide blanket, placed in the pit, and covered with trashy soil. The limits of the burial pit were established on the basis of the loose pit fill relative to the surrounding trash lenses.

BURIAL: 12-G-D2-4-2.

Component: I.

Age: 11–12 years. *Criteria:* Dental development, epiphyseal union.

Age category: 10–14.9.

Pathologies: Cribra orbitalia.

Location: Along east wall of plaza G, associated with primary plaza surface 2.

Position: Flexed, lying on right side, head to south.

Pit dimensions: Depth 42 cm below plaza surface, N-S 75 cm, E-W 43.5 cm.

Associated artifacts: Tesuque Corrugated jar sherd, leatherlike blanket.

Burial reconstruction: A pit was dug into the plaza surface, and the body was interred after having been wrapped in a hide blanket. A large sherd was placed under the left arm. The pit was then filled with trashy soil but was not covered or plastered over.

BURIAL: 12-G-D4-4-1.

Component: I.

Age: 30–36 years. *Criteria:* Pubic symphysis (McKern and Stewart 1957).

Age category: 30–34.9.

Sex: Male. *Criteria:* Pelvis.

Pathologies: Osteoma on shaft of right humerus; piece of projectile point embedded in left iliac blade; arthritic development in vertebra.

Location: Along east wall of plaza G, associated with primary plaza surface 2.

Position: Flexed, lying on face, head to south.

Pit dimensions: Depth 36 cm below plaza surface, N-S 94 cm, E-W 56 cm.

Associated artifacts: Leatherlike material, obsidian projectile point.

Burial reconstruction: A burial pit was dug into the plaza surface, and the body, apparently wrapped in some kind of leatherlike material, was interred. A clear obsidian projectile point was placed near the body. The pit was then filled with trashy soil but was not covered or plastered at plaza level.

BURIAL: 12-G-D6-4-1.

Component: I.

Age: 20– 22 months. *Criteria:* Dental development.

Age category: 1– 4.9.

Pathologies: Endocranial lesions.

Location: Along east wall of plaza G, associated with primary plaza surface 3.

Position: Flexed, lying on right side, head to east.

Pit dimensions: Depth 8 cm below plaza surface, N-S 31 cm, E-W 55 cm.

Associated artifacts: Leatherlike blanket, woven yucca-fiber mat.

Burial reconstruction: The body, wrapped in a hide or leather blanket, was laid in a pit dug into the plaza surface. Yucca mats were placed under and over the body. The pit was filled with trashy soil but was not covered or plastered at plaza level.

BURIAL: 12-G-D8-4-1.

Component: I.

Age: 4– 5 years. *Criteria:* Dental development.

Age category: 1– 4.9.

Location: Trash deposit overlying primary plaza surface 3 in plaza G, associated with plaza surface 2.

Position: Flexed, lying on face, head to east.

Pit dimensions: Pit first defined in trash lense 12 cm above plaza
   surface 3; from that point, depth was 16 cm; N-S 38 cm, E-W
   67 cm.

Associated artifacts: Leatherlike blanket, woven yucca-fiber mat, desiccated corncob.

Burial reconstruction: A pit was dug into the trash lenses overlying
   plaza surface 3, slightly intruding into that surface. A corncob
   was placed under the child's left arm, and the body was wrapped
   in a hide or leather blanket. Yucca mats were placed under and
   over the body in the grave, which was then filled with trashy soil.
   The remains of another individual (12-G-D8-4-2) intruded into
   this burial pit.

BURIAL: 12-G-D8-4-2.

Component: I.

Age: 1– 1½ months. *Criteria:* Dental development.

Age category: 0– 1.

Other skeletal information: Only cranium recovered.

Location: Trash deposit overlying plaza surface 3 along east wall of
   plaza G, associated with plaza surface 2.

Position: Head to east.

Associated artifacts: Remnants of leatherlike material.

Burial reconstruction: A burial pit was dug into the trash lenses overlying primary plaza surface 3, intruding upon burial 12-G-D8-4-1.
   The body of the infant was probably wrapped in a hide blanket
   before burial, and the pit was filled with the surrounding trashy
   soil. Disturbance prohibited complete recovery of this individual,
   and no pit dimensions were determinable.

BURIAL: 12-G-D8-4-3.

Component: I.

Age: 10– 11 months. *Criteria:* Dental development.

Age category: 0– 1.

Other skeletal information: Left neural arches of the second and third
   cervical vertebrae fused, right arches malformed.

Pathologies: Endocranial lesions.

Location: Along east wall of plaza G, associated with primary plaza
   surface 3.

Position: Flexed, lying on face, head to south.

Pit dimensions: Depth 13 cm below plaza surface, N-S 52 cm, E-W 32 cm.

Associated artifacts: Leatherlike material, woven yucca-fiber mat.

Burial reconstruction: A pit was dug into the plaza surface and the bottom lined with a yucca mat. The body of the infant, wrapped in a hide or leather blanket, was placed in the pit and covered with another mat. The pit was then filled with trashy soil but was not covered or plastered at plaza level.

BURIAL: 12-G-ST7-2-10.

Component: I.

Age: 1– 1½ months. *Criteria:* Dental development.

Age category: 0– 1.

Pathologies: Porotic hyperostosis.

Location: Along east wall of plaza G, associated with primary plaza surface 2.

Position: Lying on right side, head to north.

Pit dimensions: Depth 20 cm below plaza surface, N-S 36 cm, E-W 28 cm.

Burial reconstruction: The body was placed in a pit dug into the plaza surface. No grave goods were found, but the body lay on, and was entirely covered with, fine sand that could have been obtained only from a stream bed. No other mineral or organic material was mixed with this sand, and the pit was not covered or sealed.

BURIAL: 12-G-ST7-3-2.

Component: I.

Age: 2– 2¼ years. *Criteria:* Dental development.

Age category: 1– 4.9.

Location: Along east wall of plaza G, associated with primary plaza surface 3.

Position: Flexed, lying on right side, head to east.

Pit dimensions: Depth 73 cm below plaza surface, N-S 45 cm, E-W 72 cm.

Associated artifacts: Hide blanket; woven yucca-fiber mat; four bone tubes strung on a pine branch; and a solid hematite cylinder that was probably attached to the branch at one time.

Burial reconstruction: A pit was dug into the plaza surface, and the body, wrapped in both a hide or leather blanket and a yucca mat, was interred. Next to the right arm was found a slim pine branch with a bough at one end, strung with four bone tubes. At the bottom of the branch was a hematite cylinder. The burial pit was filled with trashy soil and was not covered or plastered over. Two posts from a later date slightly intruded into the upper pit fill.

BURIAL: 12-G-1C-2-2.
Component: I.
Age: Adult.
Age category: Adult, age unknown.
Other skeletal information: Only left leg recovered.
Location: Along west wall of plaza G, postdating primary plaza surface 1.
Pit dimensions: Depth 23 cm below plaza surface 1, N-S 210 cm, E-W 47 cm.
Burial reconstruction: Sometime after the abandonment of plaza G, a pit was dug through the trash deposits overlying the uppermost plaza surface, and this adult was buried. Only the articulated left leg was found, which might be accounted for by poor preservation, accidental disturbance, disinterment, or the reburial of remains from a previous interment.

BURIAL: 12-G-1C-3-1.
Component: I.
Age: Fetus. Criteria: Comparison with laboratory specimens.
Age category: 0–1.
Location: Along west wall of plaza G, associated with primary plaza surface 1.
Position: Lying on back, face up, head to north.
Associated artifacts: Carbonized Tesuque Corrugated sherd from the base of a jar.
Burial reconstruction: This individual, apparently an aborted fetus, had simply been laid on the plaza surface in the corner of a turkey pen and its body covered with a culinary jar sherd and perhaps a little dirt.

BURIAL: 12-G-2-3-14.
Component: I.
Age: Adult.
Age category: Adult, age unknown.

Sex: Female. *Criteria:* Sciatic notch, head of femur.

Pathologies: Bowing evident in the left femur and tibia.

Location: Along west wall of plaza G, associated with primary plaza surface 1.

Position: Flexed, lying on right side, head to north.

Pit dimensions: Depth 70 cm below plaza surface 1, N-S 110 cm, E-W 60 cm.

Associated artifacts: Yucca mat, wood pole or *latia*.

Burial reconstruction: A pit was dug into the plaza surface, and the body placed in it was covered with a yucca mat and a section of a wood pole or roof *latia*. The pit was filled with trashy soil and plastered with adobe at plaza level.

BURIAL: 12-G-2-3-21-1.

Component: I.

Age: 12–14 years. *Criteria:* Dental development, epiphyseal union.

Age category: 10–14.9.

Location: Southwest corner of plaza G, associated with primary plaza surface 1.

Position: Flexed, lying on right side, head to north.

Pit dimensions: Depth 30 cm, N-S 105 cm, E-W 35 cm.

Burial reconstruction: This individual was placed on three horizontal slabs in the fill just above the plaza surface. The walls of the room-blocks surrounding the plaza formed the west and south walls of the burial pit, and the north wall was a small stone wall that had already been built to enclose the corner of the plaza. The east wall of the burial consisted of four vertically placed stone slabs. The pit was filled with trashy soil. The legs of the skeleton were found disarticulated in the pit fill, apparently because of prehistoric disturbance.

BURIAL: 12-G-2-3-21-2.

Component: I.

Age: 14–15 years. *Criteria:* Dental development, epiphyseal union.

Age category: 10–14.9.

Pathologies: Severe localized periostitis on left tibia shaft; porosity evident at the distal ends of the femurs, both ends of the radius and ulna, and distal ends of the ribs; marked hypoplastic line in upper and lower incisors, upper and lower premolars, and upper first

112

molars (stress occurred at about 4 years of age); porosity evident in the vertebral bodies.

Location: Trash deposit behind a stone wall enclosing the southwest corner of plaza G, associated with primary plaza surface 1.

Position: Flexed, lying on left side, head to west.

Associated artifacts: Badly deteriorated pieces of woven material.

Burial reconstruction: A small stone wall enclosed the southwest corner of plaza G, the area behind it filled with trash and adobe rubble. The individual was buried in this fill just above the plaza surface; but no burial pit was observable, and it is not known whether the interment was made at the time the wall was built or later. A woven fiber material was found over the face and the right femur. The material near the waist may have been a small pouch.

BURIAL: 12-G-2-3-22.

Component: I.

Age: 34–39 years. *Criteria:* Pubic symphysis (Todd 1923).

Age category: 35–39.9.

Sex: Male. *Criteria:* Pelvis.

Other skeletal information: Odontoma erupted through the floor of the periform aperture on the left side.

Location: Along south wall of plaza G, associated with primary plaza surface 1.

Position: Flexed, lying on left side, head to south.

Pit dimensions: Depth 75 cm below plaza surface, N-S 112 cm, E-W 63 cm.

Associated artifacts: Clay pipe or cloud blower.

Burial reconstruction: While this plaza surface was in use, a pit was dug through it into the trash deposits below. The body was buried with a clay pipe near the right leg. The pit was filled with trashy soil and plastered with a 5-cm–thick layer of adobe at plaza level.

BURIAL: 12-G-2-3-27.

Component: I.

Age: 9½–10 years. *Criteria:* Dental development.

Age category: 5–9.9.

Other skeletal information: Bilateral auditory exotoses.

Location: Near southeast corner of plaza G, postdating primary plaza surface 1.

Position: Flexed, lying on left side, head to south.

Pit dimensions: Depth 18 cm below plaza surface, N-S 75 cm, E-W 55 cm.

Associated artifacts: Clay pot support or "fire dog," Tesuque Corrugated jar sherd, vegetal remains.

Burial reconstruction: This burial pit seemed too shallow to be associated with primary plaza surface 1, and it is likely that the pit was dug into the trash deposits overlying the plaza instead. However, no pit outline was observable in the trash layers. Some vegetal material was placed near the individual's head and covered with a culinary potsherd. In the trashy fill of the pit just above the body was placed a pot support or "fire dog."

BURIAL: 12-G-2-3-28.

Component: I.

Age: Adult. *Criteria:* Endocranial suture closure indicates 42+ years.

Age category: Adult, age unknown.

Sex: Male. *Criteria:* Pelvis.

Pathologies: Bowing of left femur and right tibia; arthritic development in vertebrae.

Location: Near southwest corner of plaza G, associated with primary plaza surface 2.

Position: Flexed, lying on right side, head to east.

Pit dimensions: Depth 45 cm below plaza surface, N-S 45 cm, E-W 80 cm.

Associated artifacts: Large Wiyo Black-on-white sherd that had been used as a scoop.

Burial reconstruction: While this plaza surface was in use, a pit was dug through it, the individual was buried, and the pit was filled with culturally sterile soil. At the level of the plaza surface, two slabs and a Wiyo Black-on-white sherd lay over the pit, partially covering it.

BURIAL: 12-G-2-3-29.

Component: I.

Age: 34–38 years. *Criteria:* Endocranial suture closure.

Age category: 35–39.9.

Sex: Female. *Criteria:* Pelvis, head of femur.

114

Pathologies: Bowing of right femur and right tibia; arthritic development in vertebrae.

Location: Southwest corner area of plaza G, associated with primary plaza surface 1.

Position: Semiflexed, lying on back, head to east.

Pit dimensions: Depth 60 cm below plaza surface, N-S 65 cm, E-W 85 cm.

Burial reconstruction: A burial pit was dug through the plaza surface into the underlying trash deposits. After placement of the body, the pit was filled with trashy soil but was not plastered or covered.

BURIAL: 12-G-2-3-35.

Component: I.

Age: 39–43 years. *Criteria:* Pubic symphysis (Gilbert and McKern 1971).

Age category: 40–44.9.

Sex: Female. *Criteria:* Pelvis, head of femur.

Pathologies: Pronounced bowing of humeri, radii, ulnas, femurs, tibias, and fibulas.

Location: Along east wall of plaza G, associated with primary plaza surface 1.

Position: Semiflexed, lying on left side, head to west.

Pit dimensions: Depth 63 cm below plaza surface, N-S 59 cm, E-W 103 cm.

Associated artifacts: Woven fiber mat.

Burial reconstruction: A pit was dug into the uppermost plaza surface, and the body was placed in it and covered with a woven fiber mat. The pit was filled with trashy soil and plastered over with 5 cm of adobe at plaza level.

BURIAL: 12-G-2-3-37.

Component: I.

Age: 35–45 years. *Criteria:* Pubic symphysis (Todd 1923).

Age category: 35–39.9.

Sex: Female. *Criteria:* Pelvis.

Pathologies: Bowing evident in the left femur and both tibias.

Location: Southeast corner of plaza G, postdating primary plaza surface 1.

Position: Semiflexed, lying on left side, head to south.

Burial reconstruction: A burial pit was probably dug through the trash deposits overlying plaza surface 1, although no pit was observed and the burial was not noted until the skeleton itself was found lying directly on the plaza surface. The remains were covered with trashy soil, presumably the pit fill.

BURIAL: 12-G-2-3-84.
Component: I.
Age: 13– 14 years. *Criteria:* Dental development.
Age category: 10– 14.9.
Location: Along west wall of plaza G, associated with primary plaza surface 1.
Position: Flexed, lying on right side, head to north.
Pit dimensions: Depth 32 cm below plaza surface, N-S 70 cm, E-W 43 cm.
Associated artifacts: Woven fiber mat, two unworked slabs, two manos.
Burial reconstruction: A pit was dug into the plaza surface and the bottom lined with a fiber mat upon which the body was placed. Four stones, two of them manos, were placed near the legs. The pit was then filled with trashy soil but was not covered or plastered at plaza level.

BURIAL: 12-G-2-3-159.
Component: I.
Age: 2– 2½ years. *Criteria:* Dental development.
Age category: 1– 4.9.
Pathologies: Porotic hyperostosis.
Location: Along east wall of plaza G, associated with primary plaza surface 1.
Position: Semiflexed, lying on face, head to south.
Pit dimensions: Depth 50 cm below plaza surface, N-S 76 cm, E-W 35 cm.
Associated artifacts: Woven yucca-fiber mat; hide or leather blanket; Santa Fe Black-on-white bowl sherd; Poge Black-on-white sherd.
Burial reconstruction: A pit was dug into the plaza surface and the bottom lined with a yucca mat. The body, wrapped in a hide blanket, was placed on the mat. Inside the blanket, a Santa Fe Black-on-white sherd covered the pelvic area, and a Poge Black-

on-white sherd was placed near the left arm. The burial pit was filled with trashy soil and was not covered or plastered over.

BURIAL: 12-G-2-3-198.
Component: I.
Age: 9– 10 months. *Criteria*: Dental development.
Age category: 0– 1.
Location: Southeast corner of plaza G, associated with primary plaza surface 3.
Position: Head to east.
Pit dimensions: Depth 27 cm below plaza surface, N-S 30 cm, E-W 65 cm.
Associated artifacts: Leatherlike blanket.
Burial reconstruction: The body, wrapped in a hide or leather blanket, was laid in a pit dug into the plaza surface. The pit was filled with trashy soil and covered with a small stone slab at plaza level. Sometime after the interment, a milling bin was built directly over the burial pit.

BURIAL: 12-G-2-4-8.
Component: I.
Age: 2– 2¼ years. *Criteria*: Dental development.
Age category: 1– 4.9.
Other skeletal information: Only cranium recovered.
Location: Along north wall of plaza G, postdating primary plaza surface 1.
Associated artifacts: Fragments of a Tesuque Corrugated bowl; another concentration of culinary sherds surrounding a Galisteo Black-on-white jar; fragments of a Santa Fe Black-on-white bowl.
Burial reconstruction: This cranium was found in trashy fill about 12 cm above the plaza surface. It lay between two stone slabs that had been set perpendicular to the north wall of the plaza about 120 cm apart. The skull was partially covered by Tesuque Corrugated sherds, and the other pottery mentioned above lay nearby. Next to the wall was a cluster of Poge Black-on-white bowl sherds. Several wood fragments were also found next to the skull, which may have been a secondary burial, since no other skeletal remains were found in this area. The burial pit was similar to that containing burial 12-G-2-4-10 directly to the west.

117

BURIAL: 12-G-2-4-10.
Component: I.
Age: 1½–2 years. Criteria: Dental development.
Age category: 1–4.9.
Pathologies: Porotic hyperostosis; slight porosity on the frontal above the nasals.
Location: Along north wall of plaza G, postdating primary plaza surface 1.
Position: Flexed, lying on right side, head to east.
Associated artifacts: Turreted shell pendant.
Burial reconstruction: The burial "pit" was formed by two stone slabs set perpendicular to the wall bordering the plaza; these were placed vertically about 120 cm apart. In the unstratified trashy fill between the slabs were the remains of the individual lying about 30 cm above the plaza surface and adjacent to the wall. A shell pendant was apparently placed with the body upon burial, and several wood fragments were found next to the body. This burial area was similar to that containing burial 12-G-2-4-8 directly to the east.

BURIAL: 12-G-2-4-12.
Component: I.
Age: 1½–2 months. Criteria: Dental development.
Age category: 0–1.
Location: Northwest corner of plaza G, associated with primary plaza surface 2.
Position: Head to west.
Pit dimensions: Depth 15 cm below plaza surface, N-S 30 cm, E-W 53 cm.
Associated artifacts: Hide or leather blanket.
Burial reconstruction: The body, wrapped in a hide blanket, was placed in a pit dug into the plaza surface. The pit was filled with trashy soil but was not covered or plastered over.

BURIAL: 12-G-2-4-14.
Component: I.
Age: 35–45 years. Criteria: Endocranial suture closure.
Age category: 35–39.9.
Sex: Male. Criteria: Pelvis, cranium.

Pathologies: Bowing evident in right femur; localized, healed exocranial periostitis; arthritic development in vertebrae.

Location: Northwest corner of Plaza G, associated with primary plaza surface 2.

Position: Flexed, lying on left side, head to east.

Pit dimensions: Depth 74 cm below plaza surface, N-S 53 cm, E-W 111 cm.

Associated artifacts: Woven yucca-fiber mat; gray variegated agate ceremonial axe with both blade surfaces exhibiting red and white pigment; a stick of wood, possibly the haft for the axe, since remnants of juniper-bark fiber binding material adhered to the axe; and some hidelike material possibly representing a bag.

Burial reconstruction: The body was placed on a yucca mat in a pit dug into the plaza surface. Next to the body was laid a ceremonial axe, which was found next to the face. A wooden stick, possibly the haft for the axe, was in front of the chest. A hide bag may also have accompanied the body. The pit was filled with trashy soil but apparently was not covered or plastered over. A turkey pen was later built over the burial pit.

BURIAL: 12-G-2-4-34.

Component: I.

Age: Adult.

Age category: Adult, age unknown.

Sex: Male. *Criteria:* Pelvis, cranium.

Location: Northwest corner of plaza G, associated with primary plaza surface 1.

Position: Flexed, lying on left side, head to east.

Pit dimensions: Depth 35 cm below plaza surface, N-S 56 cm, E-W 102 cm.

Associated artifacts: Leatherlike material, turquoise fragment.

Burial reconstruction: This individual was buried in a pit dug into the plaza surface, and placed with him was a small piece of turquoise that was found among the hand phalanges. Under the legs was some leatherlike material that might have been a blanket or perhaps some clothing. The burial pit was filled with trashy soil and was not covered or plastered at plaza level.

BURIAL: 12-G-2-4-36.

Component: I.

Age: 30– 36 years. Criteria: No marked arthritic development or tooth wear.

Age category: 30– 34.9.

Sex: Female. Criteria: Pelvis.

Location: Northwest corner of plaza G, associated with primary plaza surface 1.

Position: Flexed, lying on right side, head to south.

Pit dimensions: Depth 23 cm below plaza surface, N-S 98 cm, E-W 47 cm.

Burial reconstruction: The body was placed in a pit dug into the plaza surface along the wall of the adjacent roomblock. The pit was then filled with trashy soil but was not covered or plastered over.

BURIAL: 12-G-2-4-47.

Component: I.

Age: 2– 2½ years. Criteria: Dental development.

Age category: 1– 4.9.

Location: Northwest corner of plaza G, associated with primary plaza surface 2.

Position: Head to north.

Pit dimensions: Depth 21 cm below plaza surface, N-S 40 cm, E-W 25 cm.

Associated artifacts: Leatherlike blanket.

Burial reconstruction: A small burial pit was dug into the plaza surface between two posts that had been set into the surface near the roomblock wall. These posts defined the north and south limits of the pit. The body was placed in the grave wrapped in a hide or leather blanket, and the pit was filled with trashy soil. No covering or plastering of the pit was noted.

BURIAL: 12-G-2-4-63.

Component: I.

Age: 5– 6 years. Criteria: Dental development.

Age category: 5– 9.9.

Location: Northwest corner of plaza G, associated with primary plaza surface 3.

Position: Flexed, lying on left side, head to west.

Pit dimensions: Depth 27 cm below plaza surface, N-S 46 cm, E-W 72 cm.

Associated artifacts: Woven yucca-fiber mat, leatherlike blanket.

Burial reconstruction: A pit was dug into the plaza surface and the bottom lined with a yucca mat. The body, wrapped in a hide or leather blanket, was placed on the mat and the pit filled with trashy soil. Near the plaza surface in the pit fill were two small stone slabs covering the area of the body, but the pit was not otherwise covered or plastered over.

BURIAL: 12-G-4-61.

Component: I.

Age: 40–50. *Criteria:* Severe tooth wear, 40+.

Age category: 45–49.9.

Sex: Female. *Criteria:* Pelvis.

Pathologies: Severe localized periosteal infection of left proximal tibia shaft; arthritic development in vertebrae.

Location: Northwest corner of plaza G, associated with primary plaza surface 1.

Position: Flexed, lying on back, head to north.

Pit dimensions: Depth 52 cm below plaza surface, N-S 110 cm, E-W 50 cm.

Associated artifacts: Leatherlike material.

Burial reconstruction: The body of this adult female was placed in a pit dug into the plaza surface along the wall of the adjacent roomblock. The remains of some leatherlike material found in the area of the legs might have been a blanket or clothing. The pit was then filled with trashy soil. In the vicinity of this burial, the plaza surface was somewhat deteriorated and disturbed.

BURIAL: 12-G-5-1.

Component: I.

Age: 52–59 years. *Criteria:* Pubic symphysis (Gilbert and McKern 1971).

Age category: 50+.

Sex: Female. *Criteria:* Pelvis.

Pathologies: Arthritic development in vertebrae.

Location: Trash fill of kiva 12-G-5, associated with primary plaza surface 3.

Burial reconstruction: Sometime after the abandonment of the kiva, the depression left by the structure was used for trash deposition. In this trash fill, along the south wall of the kiva, were found the remains of this individual. No pit was observed in the fill, and the body appeared to have been disturbed prehistorically, perhaps when the surrounding soil slumped. This burial was not associated with other individuals found on the kiva floor.

BURIAL: 12-G-5-2.

Component: I.

Age: 37–42. *Criteria:* Pubic symphysis (Gilbert and McKern 1971).

Age category: 35–39.9.

Sex: Female. *Criteria:* Pelvis.

Pathologies: Arthritic development in vertebrae.

Location: Near floor of kiva 12-G-5, associated with primary plaza surface 3.

Burial reconstruction: This individual, one of as many as seven found on or near the kiva floor, lay on some midden and washed soil about 15 cm above the floor. All these individuals have been classified as accidental deaths. Stones were found directly on some of the skeletons. Secondary disturbance was indicated in three cases in which the articulated remains of only partial bodies were found.

BURIAL: 12-G-5-3.

Component: I.

Age: 45–49 years. *Criteria:* Endocranial suture closure.

Age category: 45–49.9.

Sex: Male. *Criteria:* Pelvis.

Location: Floor of kiva 12-G-5, associated with primary plaza surface 3.

Burial reconstruction: See burial 12-G-5-2. This individual lay on his stomach directly on the kiva floor, with a large stone slab on his back and another on his right leg.

BURIAL: 12-G-5-4.

Component: I.

Age: Adult.

Age category: Adult, age unknown.

Sex: Female. *Criteria:* Cranium.

Pathologies: Arthritic development on the heads of both radii and in the vertebrae.

Location: Floor of kiva 12-G-5, associated with primary plaza surface 3.

Burial reconstruction: See burial 12-G-5-2. This individual lay directly on the floor on her right side in a flexed position. A stone slab was found over the feet.

BURIAL: 12-G-5-5.

Component: I.

Age: 35–39 years. *Criteria:* Pubic symphysis (Gilbert and McKern 1971).

Age category: 35–39.9.

Sex: Female. *Criteria:* Pelvis.

Other skeletal information: Only the remains of an articulated pelvis and legs were recovered.

Location: Floor of kiva 12-G-5, associated with primary plaza surface 3.

Burial reconstruction: See burial 12-G-5-2. These fully articulated legs and pelvis were found directly on the floor of the kiva. Because burials 12-G-5-6 and 12-G-5-8 were also partial bodies and apparently female, all three of these burials together could represent one, two, or three individuals.

BURIAL: 12-G-5-6.

Component: I.

Age: 30–35 years. *Criteria:* Endocranial suture closure.

Age category: Adult, age unknown.

Sex: Female. *Criteria:* Cranium.

Other skeletal information: Only cranium recovered.

Location: Floor of kiva 12-G-5, associated with primary plaza surface 3.

Burial reconstruction: See burial 12-G-5-2. This individual was represented only by a cranium and two cervical vertebrae lying directly on the kiva floor. Together the remains numbered 12-G-5-6, 12-G-5-5, and 12-G-5-8 could represent one, two, or three individuals.

BURIAL: 12-G-5-7.

Component: I.

Age: 33–38 years. *Criteria:* Pubic symphysis (Todd 1923).

Age category: 30–34.9.

123

Sex: Male. *Criteria:* Pelvis.

Other skeletal information: Seventh cervical vertebra exhibits bilateral cervical rib.

Pathologies: Healed fracture on the distal end of the right radius; arthritic development in the vertebrae.

Location: Floor of kiva 12-G-5, associated with primary plaza surface 3.

Burial reconstruction: See burial 12-G-5-2. This individual was found lying directly on the kiva floor against the south wall, partially behind the hearth deflector. Two slabs and four smaller stones lay on the body.

BURIAL: 12-G-5-8.

Component: I.

Age: Adult.

Age category: Adult, age unknown.

Sex: Female. *Criteria:* Gracile bones.

Other skeletal information: Only right arm recovered.

Location: Floor of kiva 12-G-5, associated with primary plaza surface 3.

Burial reconstruction: See burial 12-G-5-2. This articulated right arm, found directly on the kiva floor, might be part of a single individual with the remains numbered 12-G-5-5 and 12-G-5-6, or together these remains might represent two or three individuals.

BURIAL: 12-G-6.

Component: I.

Age: Adult.

Age category: Adult, age unknown.

Other skeletal information: Only the articulated legs recovered.

Location: Trash deposit in plaza G, predating primary plaza surface 3.

Burial reconstruction: Sometime before the establishment of the earliest plaza surface in plaza G, a trash midden had been deposited. The remains of the individual were found in the midden about 60 cm below the plaza surface. No burial pit was observed. When the pit for kiva 12-G-5 was dug by the prehistoric inhabitants, this burial was disturbed, leaving only the articulated remains of the legs behind in the kiva wall.

BURIAL: 12-G-30A-2A-1.
Component: I.
Age: 20–22 months. *Criteria:* Dental development.
Age category: 1–4.9.
Location: Along south wall of plaza G, associated with primary plaza surface 1.
Position: Lying on back, head to east.
Pit dimensions: Depth 56 cm below plaza surface, N-S 30 cm, E-W 53 cm.
Associated artifacts: Leatherlike blanket.
Burial reconstruction: During the use of plaza surface 1, a pit was dug into it along the wall of the roomblock to the south. The infant was buried wrapped in a hide or leather blanket. Trashy soil filled the burial pit, which was not covered or plastered at plaza level.

BURIAL: 12-H-1-0-1.
Component: I.
Age: 35–39 years. *Criteria:* Pubic symphysis (Gilbert and McKern 1971).
Age category: 35–39.9.
Sex: Female. *Criteria:* Pelvis, cranium.
Other skeletal information: Spondylolysis and spina bifida in the fifth lumbar vertebra.
Pathologies: Arthritic development in vertebrae.
Location: Trash deposit in plaza H.
Burial reconstruction: Found during excavation in the trash fill of plaza H, this individual appeared to be either a disturbed burial that was secondarily deposited in the midden or a formal interment made in the midden but disturbed prehistorically, part of the skeleton being removed. No burial pit was observed.

BURIAL: 12-H-3-7-3.
Component: I.
Age: 2–3 weeks. *Criteria:* Comparison with laboratory specimens.
Age category: 0–1.
Pathologies: Widespread periostitis on postcranial skeleton; porosity at ends of long bone shafts.
Location: Trash deposit in plaza H.
Position: Lying on back, head to north.

Burial reconstruction: This newborn infant was buried in the trash midden plaza H; no burial pit was observed.

BURIAL: 12-K-SQ3-3-7.
Component: I.
Age: 20–24 years. *Criteria*: Dental development, epiphyseal union, pubic symphysis (Gilbert and McKern 1971).
Age category: 20–24.9.
Sex: Female. *Criteria*: Pelvis, cranium.
Other skeletal information: Ossification center missing from dens; bilateral developmental malformation of calcanei and naviculars.
Pathologies: Porosity evident in tarsals and bodies of vertebrae; large osteochondroma on posterior shaft surface of left femur.
Location: Trash fill in a borrow pit in plaza K.
Position: Flexed, lying on face, head to south.
Burial reconstruction: This individual was interred in the fill of a borrow pit while it was being used for trash deposition. Although no burial pit was observed, it was assumed that one had been dug and filled with the surrounding trashy soil.

BURIAL: 12-K-1.
Component: I.
Age: 14–15 years. *Criteria*: Epiphyseal union.
Age category: 10–14.9.
Sex: Female. *Criteria*: Sciatic notch.
Location: Trash midden along the edge of the arroyo adjacent to plaza K.
Position: Lying on right side, head to east.
Burial reconstruction: This individual was found washing out of a slightly trashy area at the edge of plaza K. Because it was lying at ground surface in an eroded area, the burial could not be tied in with surrounding stratigraphy. No artifacts or other material was found associated with the skeleton.

BURIAL: 12-K-3-III A #1.
Component: I.
Age: 1½–2 months. *Criteria*: Dental development.
Age category: 0–1.
Pathologies: Periostitis on all major bones and on internal surfaces of cranium; endocranial lesions.

126

Location: Along south wall of plaza K.

Position: Head to east.

Pit dimensions: Depth 16 cm below plaza surface, N-S 32 cm, E-W 50 cm.

Burial reconstruction: Burial pit A, dug into the surface of plaza K, contained two individuals. This infant was found in the upper pit fill above burial 2. Either the interment was made at the same time as that of burial 2, or at a later time 16 cm of fill had been removed from the pit and this individual buried. No covering or plastering of the pit at plaza level was noted.

BURIAL: 12-K-3-III A #2.

Component: I.

Age: 4– 5 months. *Criteria:* Dental development.

Age category: 0– 1.

Pathologies: Spongy hyperostosis; endocranial lesions.

Location: Along south wall of plaza K.

Position: Lying on right side, head to east.

Pit dimensions: Depth 47 cm below plaza surface, N-S 32 cm, E-W 50 cm.

Associated artifacts: Hide or leather blanket.

Burial reconstruction: See burial 12-K-3-III A #1. The body of this infant was either wrapped in or placed on a hide or leather blanket when interred in burial pit A. It was not disturbed or intruded upon by overlying burial 1. The burial pit was filled with trashy soil.

BURIAL: 12-K-4-III B.

Component: I.

Age: 10– 12 months. *Criteria:* Dental development.

Age category: 0– 1.

Pathologies: Severe, widespread porosity and rarification involving virtually the entire skeleton (only the centrums of the vertebrae did not have marked porosity); cribra orbitalia; porotic hyperostosis.

Location: Along south wall of plaza K.

Position: Flexed, lying on right side, head to east.

Pit dimensions: Depth 32 cm below plaza surface, N-S 34 cm, E-W 66 cm.

Associated artifacts: Large Pindi Black-on-white sherd.

Burial reconstruction: Burial pit B, dug into the plaza surface, either had a north wall consisting of two vertically set slabs or it abutted the slabs of another feature to the north. The slabs extended the full depth of the pit. The body of this infant was placed in the pit, which was then filled with trashy soil. In the fill just below plaza surface was a large potsherd overlying the infant's head. The pit was covered with a stone slab and was plastered over with the prepared adobe that made up the plaza surface.

BURIAL: 12-K-4-III C.
Component: I.
Age: 4½– 5 months. *Criteria:* Dental development.
Age category: 0– 1.
Pathologies: Porotic hyperostosis; endocranial lesions; porosity and rarification on rib and long bone fragments.
Location: Along south wall of plaza K.
Position: Lying on right side, head to east.
Pit dimensions: Depth 40 cm below plaza surface, N-S 27 cm, E-W 46 cm.
Associated artifacts: Hide blanket.
Burial reconstruction: Burial pit C was dug into the surface of the plaza and contained the remains of an infant that had been wrapped in a hide blanket before burial. The pit was filled with slightly trashy soil but was not covered or plastered over.

BURIAL: 12-K-6-II D.
Component: I.
Age: 30– 35 years. *Criteria:* Pubic symphysis (McKern and Stewart 1957; Todd 1923).
Age category: 30– 34.9.
Sex: Male. *Criteria:* Pelvis.
Location: Trash deposit above plaza K.
Position: Flexed, lying on back, head to east.
Associated artifacts: Large glaze-on-red bowl sherd.
Burial reconstruction: This individual was buried in a trash deposit overlying the surface of plaza K. In the area of the pelvis lay a large glaze-on-red potsherd. No burial pit was observable in the midden, but it was assumed that one had been dug, and it was designated pit D.

BURIAL: 12-K-12-IV E.
Component: I.
Age: 1– 1½ months. *Criteria:* Compared with other individuals in the collection.
Age category: 0– 1.
Pathologies: Porosity and bone rarification on ilium, ribs, and distal ends of long bones.
Location: Southwest corner of plaza K.
Position: Lying on right side, head to north.
Pit dimensions: Depth 30 cm below plaza surface, N-S 42 cm, E-W 24 cm.
Associated artifacts: Woven yucca-fiber mat.
Burial reconstruction: Burial pit E was dug into the plaza surface, intruding upon the earlier wall of an enclosure on the plaza. The body was laid on a yucca mat. The pit was then filled with fine, slightly trashy sand, and it was not covered or plastered at plaza level.

BURIAL: 12-K-12-IV F.
Component: I.
Age: 1¼– 1½ years. *Criteria:* Dental development.
Age category: 1– 4.9.
Pathologies: Porotic hyperostosis; cribra orbitalia; endocranial lesions.
Location: Southwest corner of plaza K.
Position: Lying on back, head to north.
Pit dimensions: Depth 30 cm below plaza surface, N-S 65 cm, E-W 42 cm.
Associated artifacts: Woven yucca-fiber mat.
Burial reconstruction: This infant was wrapped in a yucca mat and interred in a pit dug into the plaza surface. Burial pit F was filled with culturally sterile soil and was not covered or plastered at plaza level.

BURIAL: 12-K-15-IV G.
Component: I.
Age: 5– 5½ months. *Criteria:* Dental development.
Age category: 0– 1.
Pathologies: Spongy hyperostosis; rarification and porosity evident on long bone and rib fragments.

Location: Along west wall of plaza K.

Position: Head to south.

Pit dimensions: Depth 21 cm below plaza surface, N-S 46 cm, E-W 27 cm.

Associated artifacts: Woven yucca-fiber mat.

Burial reconstruction: The body of this infant was wrapped in a yucca mat and placed in burial pit G, dug into the plaza surface. The pit was filled with slightly trashy sand but was not covered or plastered at plaza level.

BURIAL: 12-K-16-IV-1 H.

Component: I.

Age: 18–20 years. *Criteria:* Pubic symphysis (McKern and Stewart 1957).

Age category: 15–19.9.

Sex: Male. *Criteria:* Pelvis.

Location: Along west wall of plaza K.

Position: Extended, lying on face, head to south.

Pit dimensions: Depth of formal burial pit 27 cm below plaza surface, N-S 90 cm, E-W 50 cm; pit extension 16 cm below plaza surface, adding 65 cm to length of pit.

Burial reconstruction: A normal burial pit was dug into the plaza surface, partially intruding upon a hearth constructed earlier. The body of this individual was not contained entirely within the pit, however. Instead, a shallower extension had been dug at the north end of the pit, and the individual's legs extended into that area. It is suggested that the body might have been in rigor mortis at the time of burial, so the pit had to be altered to accommodate the individual. The pit and extension were filled with trashy soil and were not covered or plastered over.

BURIAL: 12-K-3-IV I.

Component: I.

Age: 8½–9 months. *Criteria:* Dental development.

Age category: 0–1.

Pathologies: Slight periostitis, porosity, and rarification evident on long bone shafts.

Location: Along south wall of plaza K.

Position: Flexed, lying on left side, head to east.

Pit dimensions: Depth 10 cm below plaza surface, N-S 24 cm, E-W 50 cm.

Associated artifacts: Hide or leather blanket.

Burial reconstruction: The body of this infant, wrapped in a hide blanket, was placed in a pit dug into the plaza surface. The pit was then filled with trashy soil, covered with a stone slab, and plastered over with the prepared adobe that formed the plaza surface.

BURIAL: 12-K-3-IV J.

Component: I.

Age: 7–8 months. *Criteria:* Dental development.

Age category: 0–1.

Pathologies: Porotic hyperostosis.

Location: Along south wall of plaza K.

Position: Flexed, lying on face, head to east.

Pit dimensions: Depth 8 cm below plaza surface, N-S 32 cm, E-W 48 cm.

Associated artifacts: Hide or leather blanket.

Burial reconstruction: Burial pit J was dug into the plaza surface and contained the remains of an infant that had been wrapped in a hide blanket. The pit was filled with culturally sterile soil, covered with a stone slab, and plastered over with the prepared adobe surface of the plaza.

BURIAL: 12-6-6-5.

Component: I.

Age: Fetus or newborn. *Criteria:* Dental development.

Age category: 0–1.

Other skeletal information: Second and third cervical neural arches fused.

Location: Southeast corner of room 12-6-6.

Pit dimensions: Depth 15 cm below floor, N-S 23 cm, E-W 21 cm.

Burial reconstruction: Although this area of the floor of room 12-6-6 had been badly disturbed, it was clear that the infant had been buried in a subfloor pit.

BURIAL: 12-6-8-6E-3 A.

Component: I.

Age: Fetus. *Criteria:* Comparison with laboratory specimens.

Age category: 0– 1.
Location: Roof fall of room 12-6-8 (room 12-5-8 in field notes).
Burial reconstruction: This fetus was one of three recovered by screening the fill of the room. Apparently all three were aborted fetuses that had been interred in the soil covering the southeast quadrant of the roof of the second story room.

BURIAL: 12-6-8-6E-3 B.
Component: I.
Age: Fetus. *Criteria:* Comparison with laboratory specimens.
Age category: 0– 1.
Location: Roof fall of room 12-6-8.
Burial reconstruction: See burial 12-6-8-6E-3 A.

BURIAL: 12-6-8-6E-3 C.
Component: I.
Age: Fetus. *Criteria:* Comparison with laboratory specimens.
Location: Roof fall of room 12-6-8.
Burial reconstruction: See burial 12-6-8-6E-3 A.

BURIAL: 12-6-14-5-1.
Component: I.
Age: Fetus. *Criteria:* Comparison with laboratory specimens.
Age category: 0– 1.
Location: Along east wall of room 12-6-14 (room 12-5-14 in field notes).
Position: Flexed, lying on right side, head to north.
Pit dimensions: Depth 12 cm below floor, N-S 26 cm, E-W 18 cm.
Burial reconstruction: A small, basin-shaped niche was carved into the floor of room 12-6-14. This nearly full-term fetus was placed in the niche and covered with culturally sterile soil. The niche was not covered or plastered over.

BURIAL: 12-11-3A-2-2.
Component: I.
Age: 7– 8 years. *Criteria:* Dental development.
Age category: 5– 9.9.
Pathologies: Slight bowing of femurs.
Location: Plaza C, along wall of roomblock 11.

Position: Flexed, lying on left side, head to north.

Pit dimensions: Depth 45 cm below plaza surface, N-S 75 cm, E-W 33 cm.

Associated artifacts: Woven yucca-fiber mat, wood apparently remaining from a broken bow.

Burial reconstruction: A burial pit was dug into the Component I surface of plaza C and the bottom lined with a yucca mat. A child was placed in the grave with a broken wooden bow at its right side. The pit was then filled with trashy soil but was not covered or plastered over.

BURIAL: 12-11-8-2-13.

Component: I.

Age: 40–50 years. *Criteria:* Endocranial suture closure.

Age category: 45–49.9.

Sex: Female. *Criteria:* Pelvis, head of femur.

Pathologies: Severe arthritic development in vertebrae.

Location: Along east wall of room 12-11-8.

Position: Flexed, lying on left side, head to south.

Pit dimensions: Depth 52 cm below floor, N-S 82 cm, E-W 56 cm.

Associated artifacts: Tesuque Corrugated water jar, turquoise bead, corncob.

Burial reconstruction: This individual was buried in a pit dug through the floor of room 12-11-8. A corncob and a turquoise bead were placed with the body, and a pottery jar was found in the pit fill just above the chest area. The pit was filled with trashy soil but was not covered or plastered over at floor level.

BURIAL: 12-14-5-8-1.

Component: I.

Age: 5–5½ months. *Criteria:* Dental development.

Age category: 0–1.

Pathologies: Porosity on most external surfaces of cranium.

Location: North side of plaza G, beneath later room 12-14-5, associated with primary plaza surface 3.

Position: Head to south.

Pit dimensions: Depth 26 cm below floor, N-S 90 cm, E-W 50 cm.

Associated artifacts: Feather robe or blanket.

Burial reconstruction: Sometime after the abandonment of a *jacal* structure abutting roomblock 14, a burial pit was dug through the plaza G surface. The body of the infant placed in the grave had been wrapped in a robe or blanket that appeared to consist of feathers and yucca fiber. The pit was filled with trashy soil. Later remodeling and the construction of rooms 12-14-5 and 12-14-8 caused the pit and surrounding area to be plastered over with an adobe floor and the pit to be partially covered by a wall.

BURIAL: 12-15-7-5-1.
Component: I.
Age: 9–9½ months. *Criteria:* Dental development.
Age category: 0–1.
Pathologies: Periostitis on femur and tibia shafts, endocranial lesions.
Location: Southeast corner of room 12-15-7.
Position: Flexed, originally lying on left side, head to east (body slumped in grave).
Pit dimensions: Depth 11 cm below floor, N-S 31 cm, E-W 66 cm.
Associated artifacts: Hide or leather blanket, vegetal material, feathers.
Burial reconstruction: The body, wrapped in a hide blanket, was placed in a shallow pit dug into the floor of room 12-15-7. Some vegetal material (possibly yucca) was found inside the blanket near the legs, and the remains of some feathers lay in the area of the pelvis. The pit was filled with slightly trashy soil and was not covered or plastered at floor level.

BURIAL: 12-16-29-2-9.
Component: I.
Age: 26–30 years. *Criteria:* Endocranial suture closure.
Age category: 25–29.9.
Sex: Female. *Criteria:* Pelvis, gracile bones.
Pathologies: Dislocation of left femur from acetabulum distally; development of pseudo-joint just inferior to acetabulum on ventral area of ischium.
Location: South side of plaza C, in area designated 12-16-29.
Position: Flexed, lying on face, head to east.
Pit dimensions: Depth 25 cm below floor, N-S 62 cm, E-W 103 cm.
Associated artifacts: Hide blanket, vegetal material, six stones, palette slab with red stains, bark.

Burial reconstruction: The body, apparently wrapped in a hide blanket, was placed in a shallow pit dug into the plaza surface. Inside the blanket were the remains of some vegetal material, six stones in two clusters of three each, and a stone palette, all lying near the pelvis. Near the left arm was a concentration of yellow vegetal material. The body was apparently covered with pieces of bark, some bits of which were found in the trashy pit fill immediately above the skeleton. At surface level, three stone slabs were placed over the pit but did not entirely cover it. The pit was not plastered over but was partially covered by the reconstructed east-west wall of room 12-16-27.

BURIAL: 12-16-29-5-1.
Component: I.
Age: 44–54 years. *Criteria:* Pubic symphysis (Gilbert and McKern 1971).
Age category: 45–49.9.
Sex: Female. *Criteria:* Pelvis.
Location: South side of plaza C, in area designated 12-16-29.
Position: Flexed, lying on right side, head to east.
Pit dimensions: Depth 23 cm below floor, N-S 67 cm, E-W 97 cm.
Associated artifacts: Textile mat or blanket, red ocher on bones, pieces of bark.
Burial reconstruction: It appeared that the legs and feet of this individual had been painted with red ocher before burial. Paint remained on the metatarsals and phalanges of the feet, the proximal end of the tibia, and the shaft of the femur above the distal condyles. The body was then either wrapped in or covered with a textile blanket and placed in a pit dug into the plaza surface. Bark was found beneath the right leg on the floor of the pit, which was filled with trashy soil. The pit and the skeleton were later disturbed, with some burning occurring in the fill above the pelvis. It could not be determined whether the pit had been plastered at surface level.

BURIAL: 12-16-31-11-1.
Component: I.
Age: 5½–6 years. *Criteria:* Dental development.
Age category: 5–9.9.

Pathologies: Linear enamel hypoplasia evident in the primary upper
 incisors (pathology occurred during the fourth fetal month).
Location: Northeast corner of room 12-16-31.
Position: Head to east.
Pit dimensions: Depth 27 cm below floor, N-S 22 cm, E-W 64 cm.
Burial reconstruction: A burial pit was dug through the floor and its
 walls and bottom were smoothed with adobe. The body was placed
 in the pit, which was then filled with trashy soil. There was no
 indication that the pit had been covered or plastered over.

BURIAL: 12-16-36-4-1.
Component: I.
Age: 39–44 years. *Criteria:* Pubic symphysis (Todd 1923).
Age category: 40–44.9.
Sex: Male. *Criteria:* Pelvis, cranium.
Other skeletal information: Spondylolysis and spina bifida evident in
 the fifth lumbar vertebra.
Pathologies: Severe arthritic development in vertebrae.
Location: Along south wall of room 12-16-36.
Position: Flexed, lying on back, head to east.
Pit dimensions: Depth 48 cm below floor, N-S 54 cm, E-W 120 cm.
Associated artifacts: Hide blanket, fine-weave textile, yellow and white
 pigment on bones.
Burial reconstruction: Before burial, the body of this adult male was
 painted with yellow and white pigment, remains of which were
 present on the facial portion of the cranium, the forearms, and the
 legs. The body appeared to have been wrapped in a hide blanket,
 and fragments of a fine-weave textile were found inside the blanket around the legs. The pit, dug into the floor, was filled with
 trashy soil and covered with a stone slab at floor level, but it was
 not plastered with adobe.

BURIAL: 12-16-36-5-2.
Component: I.
Age: Adult.
Age category: Adult, age unknown.
Other skeletal information: Only left arm recovered.
Location: Along north wall of room 12-16-36.
Pit dimensions: Depth 30 cm below floor, N-S 53 cm, E-W 130 cm.

Burial reconstruction: A pit was dug into the floor of room 12-16-36, intruding upon a hearth, and an individual was buried. Later, the body was apparently disinterred, probably at a time when only tendons remained of the soft tissue. The left arm was left behind when the rest of the body was removed. Pieces of the hearth were arranged around the edge of the burial pit, which was filled with slightly trashy soil. It could not be determined whether the pit had ever been covered or plastered over.

BURIAL: 12-16-37-3.

Component: I.

Age: 35–39 years. *Criteria:* Pubic symphysis (Gilbert and McKern 1971).

Age category: 35–39.9.

Sex: Female. *Criteria:* Pelvis.

Pathologies: Slight arthritic lipping on the trochlear fossa of the right ulna and in the area of the acetabula; arthritic development in the vertebrae; small lytic lesion in right wing of sphenoid.

Location: On floor of room 12-16-37.

Burial reconstruction: These remains represent an accidental death rather than a formal burial. The individual, along with burial 12-16-37-4, was trapped in a collapse of the room, possibly while sleeping. The bodies had not been recovered by the prehistoric inhabitants for formal interment, and both were found extended on the floor.

BURIAL: 12-16-37-4.

Component: I.

Age: 35–39 years. *Criteria:* Pubic symphysis (Gilbert and McKern 1971).

Age category: 35–39.9.

Sex: Female. *Criteria:* Pelvis.

Other skeletal information: Cervical ribs associated with seventh cervical vertebra; spondylolysis and spina bifida in fifth lumbar vertebra.

Pathologies: Small lytic lesion in left orbit; arthritic development in vertebrae.

Location: On floor of room 12-16-37.

Burial reconstruction: Accidental death; see burial 12-16-37-3.

BURIAL: 12-16-38-6.

Component: I.

Age: 34–38 years. Criteria: Pubic symphysis (Gilbert and McKern 1971).

Age category: 35–39.9.

Sex: Female. Criteria: Pelvis.

Pathologies: Slight arthritic development in vertebrae.

Location: Component I trash deposits underlying Component II room 12-16-38.

Position: Semiflexed, lying on back, head to east.

Pit dimensions: Depth 118 cm below Component II floor, N-S 95 cm, E-W 68 cm.

Associated artifacts: Wood fragments.

Burial reconstruction: A burial pit was dug through a Component I use surface into the culturally sterile soil below. The body of this adult was buried with a wooden object placed near the right arm. The pit was filled with trashy soil from deposits associated with Component I. Later, Component II midden was deposited in this area and a Component II room constructed over the pit.

BURIAL: 12-18-6-3S-2.

Component: I.

Age: 4–5 years. Criteria: Dental development.

Age category: 1–4.9.

Pathologies: Bowing evident in right femur.

Location: Along east wall of room 12-18-6.

Position: Flexed, lying on right side, head to west.

Pit dimensions: Depth 50 cm below floor, N-S 50 cm, E-W 67 cm.

Associated artifacts: Wooden spoon, corncobs.

Burial reconstruction: This child was one of three buried in subfloor pits in room 12-18-6. At the bottom of the burial pit, next to the arms of the skeleton, was a wooden spoon lying on the remains of at least six corncobs. The pit was filled with sterile soil and was not covered or plastered over at floor level. This interment may have been made within a short time of burial 12-18-6-3S-8.

BURIAL: 12-18-6-3S-8.

Component: I.

Age: 16–18 months. Criteria: Dental development.

Age category: 1–4.9.
Location: Southeast corner of room 12-18-6.
Position: Flexed, lying on right side, head to east.
Pit dimensions: Depth 41 cm below floor; N-S 29 cm at floor level, 42 cm at base of pit; E-W 36 cm at floor level, 56 cm at base of pit.
Associated artifacts: Woven fiber mat, corncobs and other plant material, two slabs.
Burial reconstruction: This infant, one of three found in subfloor pits in room 12-18-6, was buried in a bell-shaped cist that probably was used originally for storage. The body was wrapped in a woven fiber mat, and next to the chest, inside the mat, were the remains of several corncobs and other plant material. Two slabs were placed over the body in the culturally sterile soil used to fill the pit, which was not covered or plastered at floor level. This burial may have been made within a short time of burial 12-18-6-3S-2.

BURIAL: 12-18-6-3S-15.
Component: I.
Age: 8–9 months. *Criteria:* Dental development.
Age category: 0–1.
Location: Doorway in south wall of room 12-18-6.
Position: Flexed, lying on right side, head to west.
Pit dimensions: Depth 50 cm below floor, N-S 30 cm, E-W 50 cm.
Associated artifacts: Woven fiber mat.
Burial reconstruction: This infant, one of three found in room 12-18-6, was buried in a pit dug into the floor directly in the doorway of the room. The body was wrapped in a woven fiber mat, and the pit was filled with sterile soil. A thick layer of adobe covering the pit made a bulge in the floor. This interment probably predated the other two made in the room, since neither of the other pits had been plastered over. The room apparently continued to be occupied for some time after the interment was made.

BURIAL: 12-18-8-4N-9.
Component: I.
Age: 14–16 months. *Criteria:* Dental development.
Age category: 1–4.9.
Pathologies: Cribra orbitalia; endocranial lesions.
Location: Northeast corner of room 12-18-8.

Position: Flexed, lying on left side, head to east.

Pit dimensions: Depth 58 cm below floor, N-S 48 cm, E-W 65 cm.

Associated artifacts: Hide or leather blanket, four shell disc beads.

Burial reconstruction: This burial was one of four found in subfloor pits in room 12-18-8, one in each corner. The body of the infant was wrapped in a hide blanket, and four shell beads, possibly a bracelet, were placed with the body. The beads were found inside the blanket in the area of the right wrist. The pit was filled with culturally sterile soil and, like burial 12-18-8-4S-8, was plastered over. These two burials probably predate the other two, which were not covered with plaster.

BURIAL: 12-18-8-4S-8.

Component: I.

Age: 10–11 months. *Criteria:* Dental development.

Age category: 0–1.

Pathologies: Cribra orbitalia; generalized porosity of the ends of the femurs, humeri, and the ends and medial aspect of the shafts of the tibias.

Location: Southeast corner of room 12-18-8.

Position: Flexed, lying on left side, head to east.

Pit dimensions: Depth 61 cm below floor, N-S 31 cm, E-W 47 cm.

Associated artifacts: Woven yucca-fiber mat.

Burial reconstruction: The body of this infant, wrapped in a yucca mat, was placed in a subfloor pit that was then filled with culturally sterile soil. The pit was plastered over at floor level and, with burial 12-18-8-4N-9, probably predated the unplastered pits of burials 12-18-8-VI-1 and 12-18-8-VII-1, found in the same room.

BURIAL: 12-18-8-VI-1.

Component: I.

Age: 26–30 years. *Criteria:* Endocranial suture closure.

Age category: 25–29.9.

Sex: Female. *Criteria:* Pelvis, cranium.

Pathologies: Cribra orbitalia; marked bowing in femur and tibias.

Location: Southwest corner of room 12-18-8.

Position: Flexed, lying on back, head to west.

Pit dimensions: Depth 30 cm below floor, N-S 45 cm, E-W 95 cm.

Associated artifacts: Glaze-on-red bowl sherd, clay pot support.

Burial reconstruction: This individual, one of four in room 12-18-8, was buried in a subfloor pit filled with trashy soil. Covering the pit at floor level were a stone slab, three smaller rocks, and a glaze-on-red potsherd. In the fill above the pelvis was a clay pot support or "fire dog." The pit had not been plastered over with adobe and probably postdated burials 12-18-8-4N-9 and 12-18-8-4S-8.

BURIAL: 12-18-8-VII-1.
Component: I.
Age: 7½–8 months. *Criteria:* Dental development.
Age category: 0–1.
Pathologies: Some porosity evident at the ends of the ribs, on the mandible, and on the ends of the long bones.
Location: Northwest corner of room 12-18-8.
Pit dimensions: Depth 50 cm below floor, N-S 60 cm, E-W 86 cm.
Associated artifacts: Necklace made of 177 juniper seed beads, two discoidal jet beads, a discoidal turquoise bead, two cylindrical jet beads, a triangular shell pendant, and an ovoid shell pendant fragment.
Burial reconstruction: One of four subfloor burials found in the corners of room 12-18-8, this individual was accompanied by an elaborate necklace of juniper seeds, shell, and stone. The burial pit was filled with trashy soil and was not covered or plastered over at floor level. This interment was probably the last to be made in the room.

BURIAL: 12-18-15-IN-1.
Component: I.
Age: 4–4½ years. *Criteria:* Dental development.
Age category: 1–4.9.
Pathologies: Porosity at distal ends of femurs; periostitis on left greater wing of sphenoid.
Location: Trash fill of room 12-18-15.
Position: Semiflexed, lying on right side, head to north.
Burial reconstruction: Toward the end of Component I, trash was deposited in the abandoned room 12-18-15. Three individuals and part of a fourth, probably all buried at the same time, were found in this trash fill near the present ground surface. No burial pit was observable, but it was assumed that one had been dug.

141

This child was one of three who were all very close in age at the time of death.

BURIAL: 12-18-15-IN-2.
Component: I.
Age: 2–2¼ years. *Criteria:* Dental development.
Age category: 1–4.9.
Pathologies: Slight bowing of fibula, right ulna, and right radius; porosity evident at distal ends of femurs; enamel hypoplasia evident on lower permanent dentition, with lower deciduous incisors broken at line of hypoplastic pitting.
Location: Trash fill of room 12-18-15.
Position: Semiflexed, lying on right side, head to west.
Associated artifacts: Large Galisteo Black-on-white sherd.
Burial reconstruction: See burial 12-18-15-IN-1. A large potsherd was found near the pelvis of this child.

BURIAL: 12-18-15-IN-3.
Component: I.
Age: 3–3¼ years. *Criteria:* Dental development.
Age category: 1–4.9.
Location: Trash fill of room 12-18-15.
Position: Semiflexed, lying on left side, head to west.
Burial reconstruction: See burial 12-18-15-IN-1.

BURIAL: 12-18-15-IN-4.
Component: I.
Age: 14–15 years. *Criteria:* Epiphyseal union.
Age category: Indeterminate.
Other skeletal information: Only right leg recovered.
Location: Trash fill of room 12-18-15.
Burial reconstruction: See burial 12-18-15-IN-1. This individual may have been interred at the same time as the three younger children found in the room, but most of the skeleton had eroded away, leaving only the right leg.

BURIAL: 12-18-39-IS-1.
Component: I.
Age: Adult.

Age category: Adult, age unknown.
Sex: Male. *Criteria:* Cranium.
Location: Trash fill of room 12-18-39.
Burial reconstruction: The badly broken and disarticulated remains of this adult male were recovered from the trash fill of room 12-18-39. It appeared that either the individual had been buried in the trash fill and later disturbed or a burial disturbed elsewhere had been reburied here. Because much of the fill in the room represented a collapsed second story, it is also possible that a disturbed body or skeleton had been left in the upper room prior to its collapse.

BURIAL: 12-18-39-IV-9.
Component: I.
Age: 4–5 months. *Criteria:* Dental development.
Age category: 0–1.
Pathologies: Porotic hyperostosis; porosity evident at the ends of the long bones.
Location: Southeast corner of room 12-18-39.
Position: Flexed, lying on left side, head to south.
Pit dimensions: Depth 35 cm below floor, N-S 50 cm, E-W 45 cm.
Associated artifacts: Woven yucca-fiber mat.
Burial reconstruction: A burial pit was dug into the floor of room 12-18-39 and the bottom lined with a yucca mat. The body of this infant was placed on the mat, and the pit was then filled with culturally sterile soil, covered with a stone slab, and plastered over at floor level.

BURIAL: 12-19-1-V-1.
Component: I.
Age: 22–24 years. *Criteria:* Pubic symphysis (McKern and Stewart 1957).
Age category: 20–24.9.
Sex: Male. *Criteria:* Cranium, head of femur.
Pathologies: Slight, healed scalp infection.
Location: Southeast corner of room 12-19-1.
Position: Flexed, lying on left side, head to west.
Pit dimensions: Depth 60 cm below floor, N-S 60 cm at bottom, E-W 80 cm at bottom.

Associated artifacts: The remains of the skin of a common raven and the wings of a white-necked raven; a gray chert projectile point; a brown chert projectile point; two Pedernal chert projectile points; wood fragments possibly from a bow; six hematite balls; one brown chert stone ball; a small stone square; one eagle claw; a bone awl tip; two sheets of mica with double drill holes.

Burial reconstruction: This individual was buried in a subfloor storage cist used secondarily as a burial pit. The bone awl tip and sheets of mica found near the back of the head may have been a hair ornament, and all the other artifacts listed above were found in the area of the knees. The pit was filled with trashy soil to about 22 cm below floor level and above was filled with roof and wall fall as the room deteriorated. It had not been plastered over.

BURIAL: 12-20-6-5-1.
Component: I.
Age: 14–15 years. *Criteria:* Dental development, epiphyseal union.
Age category: 10–14.9.
Sex: Female (?). *Criteria:* Pelvis.
Pathologies: Bilateral bowing evident in humeri, femurs, and tibias.
Location: Northeast corner of room 12-20-6.
Position: Flexed, lying on left side, head to east.
Pit dimensions: Depth 87 cm below floor, N-S 52 cm, E-W 98 cm.
Associated artifacts: A soft, hidelike material; black textile; dried squash; gourd rind painted with red ocher; some fiber fragments also covered with red ocher; a few calcined mammal and bird bones.

Burial reconstruction: This burial pit was dug through the lower of two floors in room 12-20-6. A textile of some sort had covered the bottom of the pit, and a piece of hide apparently had been placed under the individual's head. Some dried squash was found near the left shoulder, a painted gourd and some kind of painted fiber material to the right of the face. A few animal and bird bones also lay around the body. The pit was filled with culturally sterile soil and sometime later was covered by the second floor laid down in the room.

BURIAL: 12-21-3-III-1.
Component: I.
Age: 2½–3 years. *Criteria:* Dental development.

Age category: 1–4.9.
Location: Southeast corner of room 12-21-3.
Position: Flexed, lying on back, head to south.
Pit dimensions: Depth 8 cm below floor, N-S 58 cm, E-W 27 cm.
Burial reconstruction: A shallow pit was dug into the floor, and the child was placed into the pit and covered with trashy soil. The pit was not covered or plastered over at floor level.

BURIAL: 12-21-3-12-2.
Component: I.
Age: 8–9 months. *Criteria:* Dental development.
Age category: 0–1.
Location: Southwest corner of room 12-21-3.
Position: Head to north.
Pit dimensions: Depth 45 cm below floor, N-S 53 cm, E-W 30 cm.
Associated artifacts: Fine textile material, hide blanket, fiber mat.
Burial reconstruction: It appeared that the body of this infant had been placed on a piece of textile and then both body and textile wrapped in a hide blanket. The remains of a fiber mat were found under the cranium, as if it had covered the bottom of the burial pit, and another mat apparently lay over the body. The subfloor pit was filled with trashy soil but was not covered or plastered over. It was partially superimposed by a later wall.

BURIAL: 12-21-4-1-5.
Component: I.
Age: 2–2¼ years. *Criteria:* Dental development.
Age category: 1–4.9.
Location: Along north wall of room 12-21-4.
Position: Flexed, lying on right side, head to north.
Pit dimensions: Depth 24 cm below floor, N-S 42 cm, E-W 28 cm.
Associated artifacts: Hide blanket, cluster of Tesuque Corrugated sherds representing two jars.
Burial reconstruction: Sometime during the various building episodes that took place in roomblock 21, a subfloor pit was dug in room 12-21-4. The body of a young child, wrapped in a hide blanket, was interred in the pit. Probably at the same time, another small pit was dug adjacent to the first, and two culinary jars were placed

in it. Both pits were filled with trashy soil but were not covered or plastered over at floor level.

BURIAL: 12-21-5-1-3.
Component: I.
Age: 20–24 months. Criteria: Occipital development.
Age category: 1–4.9.
Location: Plaza D immediately outside the northeast corner of room 12-21-3.
Position: Head to north.
Pit dimensions: Depth 10 cm below plaza surface, N-S 48 cm, E-W 35 cm.
Associated artifacts: Slate pendant.
Burial reconstruction: This individual was found in a pit dug into the plaza surface, apparently predating the construction of room 12-21-3. A slate pendant was found in the pit near the body. The pit was filled with trashy soil but was not covered or plastered over. Later, a layer of ashy sand accumulated over the area, and the east wall of room 12-21-5 was built partially over the burial pit.

BURIAL: 12-C-A-2-1.
Component: II.
Age: 8–9 months. Criteria: Dental development.
Age category: 0–1.
Pathologies: Endocranial lesions; cribra orbitalia; periostitis on shaft of left tibia.
Location: Northeast corner of plaza C, associated with plaza surface 2.
Position: Flexed, lying on back, head to east.
Pit dimensions: Depth 27 cm below plaza surface, N-S 26 cm, E-W 45 cm.
Associated artifacts: Woven yucca-fiber mat, desiccated corncob.
Burial reconstruction: The body of this infant, wrapped in a yucca mat, was laid into a pit dug into the plaza surface. Inside the mat, beside the right arm, lay a corncob. The pit was filled with trashy soil but was not covered or plastered over.

146

BURIAL: 12-C-A-4-2.

Component: II.

Age: 22–24 years. *Criteria:* Pubic symphysis (McKern and Stewart 1957).

Age category: 20–24.9.

Sex: Male. *Criteria:* Pelvis.

Location: Along north wall of plaza C, associated with plaza surface 1.

Position: Flexed, lying on left side, head to east.

Associated artifacts: Large Pindi Black-on-white sherd.

Burial reconstruction: This individual was buried in a trash deposit between the Component I and Component II surfaces of plaza C. No pit was observed, but the skeleton lay 40 cm below plaza surface 1 of the Component II occupation. A large potsherd lay over the right shoulder of the individual, near the plaza surface. The burial had been intruded upon by burial 12-C-A-4-3, and it was apparently during this intrusion that the individual's cranium was removed.

BURIAL: 12-C-A-4-3.

Component: II.

Age: 16–18 months. *Criteria:* Dental development.

Age category: 1–4.9.

Location: Along north wall of plaza C, associated with plaza surface 2.

Position: Flexed, lying on back, head to west.

Associated artifacts: Woven yucca-fiber mat.

Burial reconstruction: This burial, found in the trash deposit underlying Component II plaza surface 2, postdated and intruded upon burial 12-C-A-4-2. The body was wrapped in a yucca mat and placed on four small logs presumably laid at the bottom of a pit, though no pit was observable. Three stone slabs were placed in a ring around the body. The burial was covered with dirt and turkey dung.

BURIAL: 12-C-A-6-1-1.

Component: II.

Age: 20–22 months. *Criteria:* Dental development.

Age category: 1–4.9.

Pathologies: Porotic hyperostosis.

Location: Borrow pit near north wall of plaza C.

Position: Semiflexed, lying on right side, head to east.

Associated artifacts: Woven yucca-fiber mat.

Burial reconstruction: This infant was buried in the trash fill of a borrow pit left from quarrying adobe in plaza C. The body was placed on a yucca mat, presumably in a burial pit. However, no pit outline was visible in the trash that surrounded the skeleton.

BURIAL: 12-C-A-7-1.

Component: II.

Age: 17–19 years. *Criteria:* Dental development, epiphyseal union.

Age category: 15–19.9.

Location: Along north wall of plaza C, just outside southeast corner of room 12-10-4, associated with plaza surface 4.

Position: Flexed, lying on left side, head to east.

Pit dimensions: Depth 26 cm below floor of room 12-10-4, N-S 37 cm, E-W 18 cm.

Burial reconstruction: Apparently a burial pit had been dug into a trash deposit, and when some pole or *latia* fragments and stone slabs were encountered, they were left in place and the body of this individual laid between them. The pit was then filled with trashy soil, and the area above it was disturbed sometime later.

BURIAL: 12-C-A-8-1.

Component: II.

Age: 5½–6 years. *Criteria:* Dental development.

Age category: 5–9.9.

Pathologies: Porotic hyperostosis.

Location: Along north wall of plaza C, associated with plaza surface 2.

Position: Lying on left side, head to south.

Pit dimensions: Depth 36 cm below plaza surface, N-S 55 cm, E-W 35 cm.

Associated artifacts: Leatherlike substance.

Burial reconstruction: A pit was dug into the plaza surface and the body of this child interred with some sort of leatherlike material placed over the mouth. The pit was filled with soil and turkey dung, and it was later badly disturbed by rodents.

BURIAL: 12-C-A-20-1-2.

Component: II.

Age: 44–54 years. *Criteria:* Pubic symphysis (Gilbert and McKern 1971).

Age category: 45–49.9.

Sex: Female. *Criteria:* Pelvis, head of femur.

Pathologies: Arthritic development in left tempro-mandibular joint and vertebrae.

Location: Borrow pit in plaza C.

Position: Flexed, lying on face, head to east.

Burial reconstruction: This individual was buried in the trash fill of a borrow pit left from quarrying adobe in plaza C. No burial pit was observable in the trashy soil.

BURIAL: 12-C-A-39-1.

Component: II.

Age: 52–59 years. *Criteria:* Pubic symphysis (Gilbert and McKern 1971).

Age category: 50+.

Sex: Female. *Criteria:* Pelvis.

Pathologies: Small osteoma on left supraorbital ridge; arthritic development in vertebrae.

Location: Along east wall of plaza C, associated with plaza surface 1.

Position: Flexed, lying on face, head to south.

Burial reconstruction: This individual was found in a trash deposit 50 cm below Component II plaza surface 1. It seemed that when the burial pit was dug, another burial (12-C-A-39-2) was encountered and that the pit had been terminated at that point and this individual buried above the earlier interment.

BURIAL: 12-C-A-39-2.

Component: II.

Ages: 22–26 years. *Criteria:* Pubic symphysis (McKern and Stewart 1957).

Age category: 20–24.9.

Sex: Male. *Criteria:* Pelvis.

Other skeletal information: Neural arch of cervical vertebra not fused and vertebra in two pieces; second and third cervical vertebrae fused together.

Location: Along east wall of plaza C, associated with plaza surface 1.

Position: Flexed, lying on face, head to north.

Pit dimensions: Depth 83 cm below plaza surface 1, N-S 115 cm, E-W 40 cm.

Burial reconstruction: The remains of this individual were discovered during the completion of excavation of overlying burial 12-C-A-39-1, which had disturbed the upper portion of the burial pit of specimen 12-C-A-39-2. The latter pit had been dug down to the Component I plaza surface, on which the body was placed, and was filled with trashy soil.

BURIAL: 12-C-A-39-3-3.
Component: II.
Age: 42–47 years. *Criteria:* Endocranial suture closure.
Age category: 40–44.9.
Sex: Female. *Criteria:* Pelvis.
Pathologies: Bowing evident in both femurs, both tibias, and right radius.
Location: Along east wall of plaza C, associated with plaza surface 1.
Position: Flexed, lying on face, head to east.
Pit dimensions: Depth 83 cm below plaza surface 1, N-S 45 cm, E-W 70 cm.
Associated artifacts: Woven yucca-fiber mat.
Burial reconstruction: A pit was dug into the trash deposits underlying the Component II plaza surface, extending down to the Component I surface. The body of this individual was either wrapped in or covered with a yucca mat, and the pit was filled with trashy soil mixed with turkey dung.

BURIAL: 12-C-9-1-1.
Component: II.
Age: 16–18 months. *Criteria:* Dental development.
Age category: 1–4.9.
Pathologies: Porotic hyperostosis.
Location: Borrow pit near north wall of plaza C.
Position: Flexed, lying on right side, head to east.
Associated artifacts: Necklace of three turreted shell pendants, one ovoid shell pendant, and a jet animal fetish.
Burial reconstruction: This infant was interred on an adobe wash surface in a trash-filled borrow pit. A necklace was placed around the neck and the body covered with the surrounding trashy soil. No burial pit was observed.

BURIAL: 12-10-4-6.

Component: II.

Age: 7–8 months. Criteria: Dental development.

Age category: 0–1.

Pathologies: Porotic hyperostosis; cribra orbitalia.

Location: Southwest corner of room 12-10-4.

Position: Flexed, lying on left side, head to south.

Pit dimensions: Depth 35 cm below floor, N-S 61 cm, E-W 38 cm.

Burial reconstruction: This individual was the only one found in a subfloor pit in a Component II room. The pit was filled with culturally sterile soil, and because of disturbance in the area it could not be determined whether the pit had been covered or plastered over.

ADULT ISOLATED REMAINS

COMPONENT I

Specimen Number	Skeletal Part
12-A-5 (15)	Vertebra fragment
12-A-5 (88)	Rib
12-A-5 (90)	Left first rib
12-A-5 (102)	Right first metacarpal
12-A-5 (109)	Vertebra fragment
12-A-6 (49)	Rib fragment
12-A-6 (66)	Hand phalange
12-B (7)	Rib fragment
12-B-9 (23)	Male left temporal
12-C-3-10-1	Male facial cranium
12-G-39-1	Left mandibular condyle
12-G-2A-2-1	Rib, left temporal, upper right first molar
12-G-2A-2-2	Parietal fragment
12-G-8A-2	Right radius fragment
12-G-14A-2	Premolar
12-G-14A-2 (B)	Cranial fragment
12-G-19A-2	Lumbar vertebra
12-G-25A-II	Cervical vertebra

Specimen Number	Skeletal Part
12-G-25A-III	Left calcaneus epiphysis, young adult vertebra fragment
12-G-25A-3-1	Innominate, ischium, and pubis just fusing; right third cuniform; right tibia fragment (two individuals)
12-G-27A-2	Mandible fragments, lower molar, lower premolar
12-G-36B	Left foot navicular
12-G-107B-2	Foot phalange
12-G-1C-2	Cranial fragments, lower left second molar
12-G-2C-2	Upper left first molar
12-G-20C-2	Terminal foot phalange
12-G-26C-2-1	Left talus, right calcaneus, left third metacarpal, two foot phalanges
12-G-C-37-2	Lower right first incisor, metatarsal
12-H-2-5	Upper first incisor
12-H-2-5-4	Right maxilla, upper second molar
12-H-3-5-3	Upper second premolar
12-H-3-5-5	Left capitate
12-H-3-6-5	Left parietal
12-H-4-4-5	Foot phalange
12-K-1	Hand phalange, epiphysis not fused
12-K-1	Hand phalange, proximal epiphysis not fused
12-K-6-II	Two hand phalanges, right and left capitate, right second metacarpal, right fourth metacarpal, right greater multangular, right pisiform (one individual)
12-K-14-II & III	Sacral fragment
12-K-16-IV-1	First metacarpal, hand phalange
12-6-7-IVE-1	Cranial fragment
12-7-7-2 (5)	Molar enamel fragment
12-9-7-3	Left innominate fragment
12-9-7-3 (7)	Lower molar
12-9-7-3 (13)	Innominate fragment
12-9-7-3 (41)	Vertebra fragment

Specimen Number	*Skeletal Part*
12-11-8-2-1 (1)	Right and left hamate, right and left navicular, right lesser multangular, left lunate, second and third metacarpals, vertebra fragment, sacral fragment, miscellaneous fragments (one individual)
12-11-8-2-2	Male(?) manubrium
12-11-10	Left patella, fifth metatarsal
12-11-11	Female left innominate fragment
12-12-4-9	Cranial fragment
12-15-7-1 (1)	Fifth sacral segment
12-16-7-1 (68)	Lesser multangular
12-16-27-2 (8)	Second cervical vertebra, left ossification center of dens missing
12-16-27-2 (24)	Occipital fragment
12-16-27-3-1	Female(?) cranial vault fragment, mandible fragments
12-16-27-4 (2)	Foot phalange
12-16-29-0 (2)	Cervical vertebra
12-16-29-1 (5)	Sacral unit
12-16-29-1	Three thoracic vertebrae, epiphyseal rings not fused
12-16-29-1 (49)	Left calcaneus
12-16-29-2-5	Developing tooth crown
12-16-29-6 (2)	Right first metacarpal, distal epiphysis just fusing
12-16-29-6 (3)	Right first metatarsal
12-16-29-6 (6)	Vertebra fragment
12-16-29-6 (7)	Vertebra fragment
12-16-29-6 (10)	Vertebra fragment
12-16-29-6 (12)	Vertebra fragment
12-16-39-1 (3)	Left first, second, third, and fourth metatarsals (one individual)
12-16-36-2 (18)	Hand phalange
12-16-36-2 (17)	Tarsal
12-16-36-2 (97)	Foot phalange
12-16-36-2 (99)	Right fifth metatarsal
12-16-36-2 (112)	Foot phalange

Specimen Number	Skeletal Part
12-16-37-2 (27)	Sphenoid fragment
12-16-37-3 (1)	Cervical vertebra
12-16-37-3 (2)	Foot phalange
12-16-37-3 (3)	Hand phalange
12-16-37-3 (4)	Terminal hand phalange
12-18-7-2 (14)	Left first metatarsal
12-18-7-IV-4	Enamel fragments
12-18-7-V-5	Enamel fragments
12-18-9-2N-2	Left half of mandible with first and second premolars and first and second molars; metacarpal
12-18-39-2N-13	Left second, third, and fourth metatarsals (one individual)
12-18-49-8N&S	Sacral fragment
12-21-0	Left ulna
12-24-3-II (2)	First metacarpal fragment
12-24-3-4	Right talus, right calcaneus, right patella

COMPONENT II

12-C-0	Ulna fragment
12-C-3-9	Left temporal fragment
12-C-4-9	Long bone fragment
12-C-A-14	Right third metacarpal, left foot navicular
12-C-A-35-1	Cervical vertebra
12-C-A-9	Tooth
12-C-A-20-1-1	Left fibula fragment, left tibia fragment
12-C-3B-2-1	Fibula
12-C-3C-2-7	Frontal fragments
12-C-3C-2-8	Right maxilla and cranial fragments
12-9-0	Right second metacarpal
12-9-13-IIW	Upper right first incisor
12-9-10-2S	Right hamate
12-9-10-IIS	Upper right premolar
12-9-10-IIN	Cervical vertebra

Specimen Number	Skeletal Part
12-9-11-IN	Upper right first premolar
12-9-12-IIW	Lower right first incisor
12-10-5-2N	Thoracic vertebra, left foot navicular (adolescent); thoracic vertebra (centrum and neural arches just fusing)
12-10-6	Left fifth metatarsal
12-16-10-1 (4)	First cervical vertebra
12-16-19-1 (5)	Foot phalange
12-16-19-12 (3)	Sternum fragment
12-16-20-4 (14)	Lower premolar
12-16-22-3 (1)	Right fifth metacarpal

ISOLATED REMAINS, IMMATURE INDIVIDUALS

COMPONENT I

Specimen Number	Skeletal Part
12-A-5 (107)	Temporal fragment (2+ years)
12-A-5 (110)	Vertebra centrum (10–11 years)
12-A-6 (63)	Cranial fragment (approximately 2 years)
12-D-32	Parietal fragments (less than 14 months)
12-F-3-B	Right scapula, rib, neural arch of thoracic vertebra (one individual, 14–16 months)
12-G-2A-2	Left clavicle (2 years)
12-G-3A-2	Centrum (approximately 12–18 months)
12-G-3A-2-1	Right tibia, two ribs, right ischium, sacral unit, cranial fragments, three cervical vertebrae arches, one thoracic vertebra neural arch (one individual, 2–2¼ years)
12-G-9A-2	Left femur (8+ fetal months)
12-G-15A-2	Metacarpal (6+ years)
12-G-21A-2	Humerus (birth)

Specimen Number	Skeletal Part
12-G-25A-2	Right fourth metacarpal, distal epiphysis not fused
12-G-25A-III	Left calcaneus; first, second, and third foot multangulars (one individual, 10 years); centrum, hand phalange (one individual, slightly younger than 10 years)
12-G-2-29A-2	Sacral arch and centrum fragments, right ilium (one individual, 2 years)
12-G-31A-2	Metacarpal (4–5 years)
12-G-34A-2-10	Left humerus, left tibia fragment, left half of mandible, deciduous incisors (one individual, 1½ years)
12-G-35A-2	Left femur, tibia (one individual, 10 months)
12-G-40B-2	Foot phalange (approximately 3 years)
12-G-7C-2	Left scapula (birth)
12-G-C31-2	Cranial fragment, upper left deciduous second molar (10 months)
12-G-C36-2	Right radius, rib fragment, right parietal fragment (18 months)
12-G-D10-2	Left half mandible (5½ months)
12-G-4-60-2	First rib, hand phalange (approximately 20 months)
12-G-5-I	Right humerus (approximately 5 months)
12-H-2-5-4	Deciduous upper second molar
12-K-6A-3	Vertebra fragment (4 months)
12-K-14-IV	Neural arch of cervical vertebra (12–18 months)
12-K-14-IV	Ribs (approximately 2 years)
12-K-15-II&III	Rib, sacral unit, metatarsals (approximately 6 months)
12-K-15-4-2	Rib (approximately 1 year)
12-K-16-II	Rib (approximately 6 months)
12-K-16-II&III	Left half mandible, rib (2 months); radius fragment, rib (birth)
12-K-16-IV	Left clavicle, right scapula, right tibia,

Specimen Number	Skeletal Part
	neural arch of second cervical vertebra, ribs (one individual, 3 months); left clavicle (5 years)
12-K-16-IV-1	Left scapula, occipital (birth)
12-10-Test pit 6	Deciduous lower molar, cranial fragments (6 months)
12-16-7-1 (46)	Foot phalange (approximately 2 years)
12-16-29-1 (121)	Right clavicle (approximately 6 months)
12-16-31-3 (6)	Hand phalange (approximately 5 years)
12-16-36-1 (30)	Malar (approximately 6–9 months)
12-18-15-I	Left tibia fragment, distal femur epiphysis, femur fragments, rib, phalanges, miscellaneous fragments (one individual, 2 years)
12-18-15-I	Metacarpal (6–8 years)

COMPONENT II

12-C-A-6-1	Neural arch of thoracic vertebra, miscellaneous fragments (16–18 months)
12-C-A-20-1	Left tibia (3–4 months)
12-C-A-35	Right petrous (1 year); tibia fragment, ribs, two thoracic vertebrae (7 years)
12-9-10-IIN	Left radius (12–18 months)
12-9-10-2N	Cervical vertebra, thoracic vertebra, centrum (12–14 months)
12-9-10-2S	Vertebra fragment (3 years); right tibia (birth)
12-9-11-IIIN	Right femur (birth)
12-9-11-IIIS	Upper right deciduous first incisor (3+ years)
12-16-5-6 (4)	Right fifth metatarsal (8–10 years)
12-16-16-2 (24)	Cranial fragment (14–18 months)

Appendix E

SUMMARY OF GRAVE ACCOUTREMENTS

In Table 33, only individuals recovered from formal burials and accompanied by grave accoutrements are listed. Those lacking grave goods or found as victims of accidents are excluded. Abbreviations used in the table are:

1. Pot or sherd
    P   Painted sherd or pot
    C   Culinary sherd or pot
2. Plant remains
    CC   Corncob
    S   Squash
    X   Present but unidentifiable
3. Other categories
    X   Item present

TABLE 33.
Summary of grave accoutrements.

COMPONENT I

Age Category/ Specimen Number	Age	Sex	Hide Blanket	Yucca Mat	Pot or Sherd	Plant Remains	Other Items
0–1 year							
12-G-B110-4	2½–3 months	—	x	x	—	—	
12-G-D2-4-1	1–1½ months	—	x	—	—	—	
12-G-D8-4-2	1–1½ months	—	x	—	—	—	
12-G-D8-4-3	10–11 months	—	x	x	—	—	
12-G-1C-3-1	Fetus	—	—	—	C	—	
12-G-2-3-198	9–10 months	—	x	—	—	—	
12-G-2-4-12	1½–2 months	—	x	—	—	—	
12-K-3-III A #2	4–5 months	—	x	—	—	—	
12-K-4-III B	10–12 months	—	—	—	P	—	
12-K-4-III C	4½–5 months	—	x	—	—	—	
12-K-12-IV E	1–1½ months	—	—	x	—	—	
12-K-15-IV G	5–5½ months	—	—	x	—	—	
12-K-3-IV I	8½–9 months	—	x	—	—	—	
12-K-3-IV J	7–8 months	—	x	—	—	—	
12-14-5-8-1	5–5½ months	—	—	—	—	—	Feather Robe
12-15-7-5-1	9–9½ months	—	x	—	—	x	Feathers
12-18-6-3S-15	8–9 months	—	—	x	—	—	
12-18-8-4S-8	10–11 months	—	—	x	—	—	Necklace with jet, turquoise, shell and juniper seed beads
12-18-8-VII-1	7½–8 months	—	—	—	—	—	
12-18-39-IV-9	4–5 months	—	—	x	—	—	
12-21-3-12-2	8–9 months	—	x	x	—	—	Fabric

Age Category/Specimen Number	Age	Sex	Hide Blanket	Yucca Mat	Pot or Sherd	Plant Remains	Other Items
1–4.9 years							
12-G-B110-2	4–5 years	—	x	x	—	CC	
12-G-B110-3	16–18 months	—	x	x	—	—	
12-G-D6-4-1	20–22 months	—	x	x	—	CC	
12-G-D8-4-1	4–5 years	—	x	x	—	CC	
12-G-ST7-3-2	2–2¼ years	—	x	x	—	—	Pine branch with four bone tubes and hematite cylinder
12-G-2-3-159	2–2½ years	—	x	x	P	—	
12-G-2-4-8	2–2¼ years	—	—	—	P	—	
12-G-2-4-10	1½–2 years	—	—	—	—	—	Shell pendant
12-G-2-4-47	2–2½ years	—	x	—	—	—	
12-G-30A-2A-1	20–22 months	—	x	x	—	—	
12-K-12-IVF	1¼–1½ years	—	—	x	—	—	
12-18-6-3S-2	4–5 years	—	—	—	—	CC	Wooden spoon
12-18-6-3S-8	16–18 months	—	—	x	—	CC	
12-18-8-4N-9	14–16 months	—	x	—	—	—	4 shell beads
12-18-15-IN-2	2–2¼ years	—	—	—	P	—	
12-21-4-1-5	2–2¼ years	—	x	—	C	—	
12-21-5-1-3	20–24 months	—	—	—	—	—	Slate pendant
5–9.9 years							
12-G-2-3-27	9½–10 years	—	—	—	C	x	Pot support
12-G-2-4-63	5–6 years	—	x	x	—	—	
12-11-3A-2-2	7–8 years	—	—	x	—	—	Wooden bow

161

Age Category/ Specimen Number	Age	Sex	Hide Blanket	Yucca Mat	Pot or Sherd	Plant Remains	Other Items
10–14.9 years							
12-G-2-3-21-2	14–15 years	—	—	—	—	—	Material sack; yucca material
12-G-2-3-84	13–14 years	F	—	x	—	—	Two manos
12-G-D2-4-2	11–12 years	—	x	—	C	—	
12-20-6-5-1	14–15 years	F	—	—	—	S	Rabbit skin; painted gourd; black textile
15–19.9 years							
12-C-A-12-1	16–18 years	M	—	x	—	—	
20–24.9 years							
12-19-1-V-1	22–24 years	M	—	—	—	—	*
25–29.9 years							
12-G-B111-4	25–28 years	M	—	x	—	x	Six stones; palette slab
12-16-29-2-9	26–30 years	F	x	—	—	—	
12-18-8-VI-1	26–30 years	F	—	—	P	—	
30–34.9 years							
12-G-D4-4-1	30–36 years	M	x	—	—	—	Obsidian point
12-K-6-IID	30–35 years	M	—	—	P	—	

*Recovered with burial 12-19-1-V-1 were the skin of a common raven, wings of a white-necked raven, four arrowpoints, wood fragments (possibly a bow), seven stone balls, a small stone square, the claw of an eagle, two sheets of mica, and a bone awl tip.

Appendix E

Age Category/Specimen Number	Age	Sex	Hide Blanket	Yucca Mat	Pot or Sherd	Plant Remains	Other Items
35–39.9 years							
12-G-2-3-22	34–39 years	M	—	—	—	—	Clay pipe
12-G-2-4-14	35–45 years	M	—	x	—	—	Leather bag; ceremonial axe
12-16-38-6	34–38 years	F	—	—	—	—	Wood fragments
40–44.9 years							
12-G-2-3-35	39–43 years	F	—	x	—	—	—
12-16-36-4-1	39–44 years	M	x	—	—	—	Fabric; body paint
45–49.9 years							
12-G-4-61	40–50 years	F	x	—	—	—	—
12-11-8-2-1-3	40–50 years	F	—	—	C	CC	Turquoise bead
12-16-29-5-1	44–54 years	F	—	x	—	—	Body paint; bark
Adult, Age Unkown							
12-G-2-3-14	?	F	—	x	—	—	Wooden *latia*
12-G-2-3-28	?	M	—	—	P	—	—
12-G-2-4-34	?	M	x	—	—	—	Turquoise fragment

COMPONENT II

Age Category/Specimen Number	Age	Sex	Hide Blanket	Yucca Mat	Pot or Sherd	Plant Remains	Other Items
0–1 year							
12-C-A-2-1	8–9 months	—	—	x	—	CC	

Age Category/ Specimen Number	Age	Sex	Hide Blanket	Yucca Mat	Pot or Sherd	Plant Remains	Other Items
1–4.9 years							
12-C-A-4-3	16–18 months	—	—	x	—	—	
12-C-A-6-1-1	20–22 months	—	—	x	—	—	
12-C-9-1-1	16–18 months	—	—	—	—	—	Necklace with shell beads and jet fetish
5–9.9 years							
12-C-A-8-1	5½–6 years	—	—	—	—	—	Leather strip
20–24.9 years							
12-C-A-4-2	22–24 years	M	—	—	P	—	
40–44.9 years							
12-C-A-39-3-3	42–47 years	F	—	x	—	—	

Appendix F

SUMMARY OF SKELETAL PATHOLOGIES

In the following table, only individuals exhibiting some kind of pathology are listed. Arthritis, a common pathological condition seen in the Arroyo Hondo adult skeletons, is not included here because the focus of the pathology analysis was dietary stress rather than patterns of the normal aging process.

TABLE 34.
Summary skeletal pathologies.

Age Category/ Specimen Number	Age	Sex	Porotic Hyperostosis	Endocranial Lesions	Cribra Orbitalia	Porosity	Bowing	Other Pathologies
COMPONENT I								
0–1 year								
12-G-B110-4	2½– 3 mo.							Widespread periostitis
12-G-D2-4-1	1– 1½ mo.				X	X	X	
12-G-D8-4-3	10– 11 mo.		X					
12-G-ST7-2-10	1– 1½ mo.			X				Widespread periostitis
12-H-3-7-3	2– 3 wk.			X				Widespread periostitis
12-K-3-III A1	1½– 2 mo.		X			X		
12-K-3-III A2	4– 5 mo.		X			X		
12-K-4-III B	10– 12 mo.		X		X	X		
12-K-4-III C	4½– 5 mo.			X		X		
12-K-12-IV E	1– 1½ mo.		X					
12-K-15-IV G	5– 5½ mo.							
12-K-3-IV I	8½– 9 mo.		X					
12-K-3-IV J	7– 8 mo.					X		
12-14-5-8-1	5– 5½ mo.							
12-15-7-5-1	9– 9½ mo.			X				
12-18-8-4S-8	10– 11 mo.				X	X		
12-18-8-VII-1	7½– 8 mo.					X		
12-18-39-IV-9	4– 5 mo.		X			X		

Age Category/Specimen Number	Age	Sex	Porotic Hyperostosis	Endocranial Lesions	Cribra Orbitalia	Porosity	Bowing	Other Pathologies
1–4.9 years								
12-G-D6-4-1	20–22 mo.			X				
12-G-2-3-159	2–2½ yr.		X					
12-G-2-4-10	1½–2 yr.		X					
12-K-12-IVF	1¼–1½ yr.		X	X	X			
12-18-6-3S-2	4–5 yr.		X	X				
12-18-4N-9	14–16 mo.						X	
12-18-15-IN-1	4–4½ yr.					X		
12-18-15-IN-2	2–2¼ yr.					X	X	
5–9.9 years								
12-G-2-3-27	9½–10 yr.							
12-11-3A-2-2	7–8 yr.						X	Auditory exotoses
10–14.9 years								
12-G-2-3-31-2	14–15 yr.							Localized periostitis
12-G-D2-4-2	11–12 yr.				X	X		
12-20-6-5-1	14–15 yr.	F					X	
15–19.9 years								
12-C-A-12-1	16–18 yr.	M					X	
20–24.9 years								
12-K-SQ3-3-7	20–24 yr.	F						Osteochondroma
12-19-1-V-1	22–24 yr.	M						Localized osteomyelitis

Age Category/Specimen Number	Age	Sex	Porotic Hyperostosis	Endocranial Lesions	Cribra Orbitalia	Porosity	Bowing	Other Pathologies
25–29.9 years								
12-G-B111-4	25–28 yr.	M					X	Osteoma
12-16-29-2-9	26–30 yr.	F						Dislocation
12-18-8-VI-1	26–30 yr.	F			X		X	
30–34.9 years								
12-G-D4-4-1	30–36 yr.	M						Osteoma; embedded projectile point
12-G-5-7	33–38 yr.	M						Healed fracture
35–39.9 years								
12-G-2-3-29	34–38 yr.	F					X	
12-G-2-3-37	35–45 yr.	F					X	Localized periostitis
12-G-2-4-14	35–45 yr.	M					X	Localized lytic lesion
12-16-37-3	35–39 yr.	F						Localized lytic lesion
12-16-37-4	35–39 yr.							
40–44.9 years								
12-G-2-3-35	39–43 yr.	F					X	
45–49.9 years								
12-G-4-61	40–50 yr.	F						Localized osteomyelitis
50+ years								
12-D-2-2-1	52–59 yr.	F						Localized periostitis
Adult, Age Unknown								
12-G-2-3-14		F					X	
12-G-2-3-28	42+ yr.(?)	M					X	

168

Age Category/Specimen Number	Age	Sex	Porotic Hyperostosis	Endocranial Lesions	Cribra Orbitalia	Porosity	Bowing	Other Pathologies
COMPONENT II								
0–1 year								
12-C-A-2-1	8–9 mo.			X	X			Localized periostitis
12-10-4-6	7–8 mo.		X		X			
1–4.9 years								
12-C-A-6-1-1	20–22 mo.		X					
12-C-9-1-1	16–18 mo.		X					
5–9.9 years								
12-C-A-8-1	5½–6 yr.		X					
40–44.9 years								
12-C-A-39-3-3	42–47 yr.	F					X	
50+ years								
12-C-A-39-1	52–59 yr.	F						Osteoma

Appendix G

ARROYO HONDO
POPULATION AFFINITIES

James Mackey

Ancestral biological similarity is undoubtedly reflected in discrete skeletal traits, and the study of these traits can be used to estimate intergroup relationships. Relative similarity between two or more skeletal series in the incidence of discrete cranial traits can be interpreted as evidence of biological and/or historical relatedness. In this paper, a multivariate statistical analysis of discrete cranial traits is used to study the population affinities of skeletal series from Arroyo Hondo and other probable ancestral Tewa-Tano Puebloan sites.

The rationale for using nonmetric cranial traits to estimate genetic population distance is based on their discrete distribution: presence or absence. Presumably such an expression is likely to be controlled by a small number of genes. If more than a few genes were involved, a continuous distribution would probably result. While environmental factors such as nutrition may have some effect on the expression of discrete traits, genetic control seems to be more important (R. J. Berry 1968:103–11; A. C. Berry 1974:345; Corruccini 1974:425). Because metric traits have a continuous distribution, their expression may be influenced by a larger number of genes (they are polygenic traits) and to a greater degree by environment.

On the other hand, the use of metric data to estimate biological distance may be preferable to studying discrete traits or single gene polymorphisms such as blood groups and serums. This is because polygenic traits are less susceptible to random genetic drift, which is extremely important in explaining the great amount of genetic variability in single gene polymorphisms in small, isolated populations such as Puebloan villages (Bielicki 1962:3; Angel 1966:536; Cavalli-Sforza 1969; Neel and Ward 1970; Rhoads and Friedlaender 1975; Roychoudhury 1975). Whether discrete or continuous traits are preferable for documenting population affinities cannot be resolved here; both approaches can be defended. However, the small number of adult crania from Arroyo Hondo would make questionable any estimate of population affinities based on continuous traits. Because of the small sample size, only discrete cranial traits are used to estimate Arroyo Hondo's population affinities.

METHODOLOGY AND STATISTICS

The analysis was based on the presence or absence of 20 discrete cranial traits, which are listed in Table 36. Originally, as many as 30 discrete traits were scored for each cranium. However, because the populations were studied over a period of almost two years, a number of series that were scored early in the study were later rescored to see if the data were reproducible. It was found that some of the population means of the discrete traits could not be reliably reproduced. Also, poor preservation resulted in inadequate sample sizes for a number of populations. Therefore, the standard list of 30 traits (Berry and Berry 1967) was reduced to 20. The reliability of the biological distance estimates could only have increased from shortening the list.

Several researchers have investigated the correlation between discrete traits and found it to be low (Berry and Berry 1967:373–75; Corruccini 1974:430–31). In this study, because all skulls were scored by a single investigator, interobserver error was controlled. Because only adult crania were included, variability in the expression of discrete traits with age (Corruccini 1974:430–31) was also minimized.

Though the possibility of sexual differences in the expression of some of these traits is suspected (Berry and Berry 1967:370; Corruccini 1974:428–32), the analysis was not limited either to males or females.

The resultant reduction in sample sizes would have led to problems far outweighing the possibility of one or more populations having a disproportionate frequency of one sex and therefore a biased population estimate of a trait's frequency. Most important, the reduced sample size would have increased random errors.

Lateral traits may occur on both sides of the skull. Usually the sample incidence of such traits represents the total number of occurrences (A. C. Berry 1974:348), but skulls scored in this study were considered positive expressions if one or both lateral traits were present. The important point is not which of the two approaches is used but that the chosen approach is used consistently to score lateral traits in all populations.

The mean measure of divergence (A. C. Berry 1974; Berry and Berry 1967; R. J. Berry 1968), a multivariate distance statistic, was used to quantify the biological distance between populations. The statistic changes the percentage of each variate into an angular transformation measured in radians. The sum of the squared absolute differences between each pair of transformed measurements from two populations is divided by the number of discrete traits scored, and the variance due to sampling error fluctuation is subtracted. The mean measure of divergence is the statistic most commonly used to measure population distance by means of discrete data.

For several reasons, no tests were made of the statistical significance of all the 91 estimates of biological distance in Table 37. Most important, statistically significant differences and biologically significant differences are not necessarily the same thing. That many of the pairwise population distance estimates are statistically significant does not necessarily mean that the samples were drawn from two biologically distinct populations. This statement is especially true for Puebloan populations, which are largely genetically homogeneous relative to non-Puebloan southwestern populations, at least for metric and discrete traits. A large amount of the intervillage genetic variability that exists, at least in single-gene polymorphisms such as blood groups, is undoubtedly due to genetic drift, as it is among other nonindustrial populations with subsistence agriculture or hunting-gathering adaptations (Cavalli-Sforza 1969; Neel and Ward 1970; Roychoudhury 1975; Rhoads and Friedlaender 1975). In addition, statistical significance depends on sample size, variability in expression of a given trait within a sample, and so forth.

POPULATION SAMPLES

Map 2 shows the 14 archaeological sites from which the skeletal materials were obtained and the geographic distribution of the late prehistoric and early historic ethnolinguistic groups in the Pueblo Southwest. Sites were assigned to known ethnolinguistic groups on the basis of similarities in ceramics and architecture, continuous spatial distribution, continuity into historic times, and historic documentation. A site's ethnolinguistic assignment generally agrees with the consensus of southwestern anthropological opinion.

For example, Giusewa is one of eight sites in the Jemez River area, all of which have extensive cultural similarities that could only have resulted from occupation by a single ethnolinguistic-genetic group or "tribe." This interpretation is supported by historical documentation: "Forty leagues to the northeast there is the province of Hemes, with seven pueblos" (Castañeda 1940:254). Though this classic anthropological view of the tribe (Romney 1957) is a simplification, there is no doubt that the cultural similarities between the Jemez sites would result from more frequent *intra*tribal, intervillage marriage and contact than *inter*tribal, intervillage marriage and contact.

In Table 35 are listed the sites used in this study, their probable

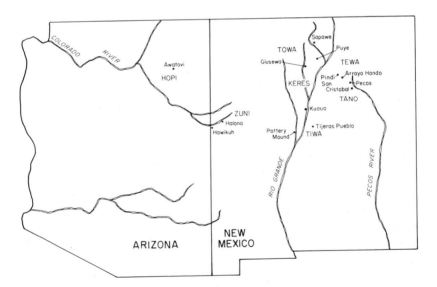

MAP 2.   Locations of sites included in the population affinity analysis.

174

TABLE 35.
Information about archaeological sites included in this study.

Site	Skeletal Sample Size	Affiliation	Date of Occupation
Guisewa	41	Jemez Towa	Prehistoric–17th century[1]
Puye	74	Tewa	15th–17th century[2]
			Middle–late 16th century[1]
Sapawe	29	Tewa	15th century[2]
Arroyo Hondo	33	Tewa-Tano	A.D. 1300–1425
Pindi	28	Tewa-Tano	A.D. 1250–1350[3]
San Cristobal	38	Tano	Late 14th–17th century[4]
Pecos	21	Towa or Tewa-Tano	A.D. 1300–1600[4]
Pecos Mission	24	Towa or Tewa-Tano	Historic–A.D. 1838[4]
Kuaua	40	Southern Tiwa	14th century–historic[1]
Pottery Mound	37	Southern Tiwa	A.D. 1325–1525[5]
			14th–17th century[6]
Tijeras Pueblo	18	Southern Tiwa	14th century[1]
Hawikuh	61	Zuni	Prehistoric–A.D. 1680[7]
			Late 14th century-historic[8]
Halona	17	Zuni	Late prehistoric–A.D. 1680[7]
Awatovi	38	Hopi	13th–18th century[8]
			Late prehistoric–A.D. 1700[7]

[1]Robinson, Hannah, and Harrill 1972
[2]Mera 1934
[3]Stallings 1937;Smiley 1951;
  Stubbs and Stallings 1953
[4]Robinson, Harrill, and Warren 1973
[5]Schorsch 1956
[6]Mera 1940
[7]Hodge 1907
[8]Bannister, Hannah, and Robinson 1970

linguistic-cultural affiliations, their dates of occupation, and the size of each skeletal sample. In population affinity studies of this type, the skeletal series should be approximately contemporaneous. Considering the difficulties of accurately dating archaeologically recovered materials, these skeletal series seem to meet this requirement. One could be more rigorous by including only the sites that could be shown to be definitely contemporaneous by tree-ring dating, historical documentation, or possibly ceramic seriation. However, it would be hard to find a large number of sites that were contemporaneous throughout their entire duration of occupation and even harder to find a number of such sites that had sufficient burial data and could also be associated with known linguistic or ethnic groups. Within the limits of archaeological data, the sites used here are the best sample of which I am aware.

As previously stated, there is little doubt that Guisewa is an ancestral Towa site. Puye and Sapawe, culturally similar to one another, are situated in an area historically documented as being occupied by the Tewas. The Arroyo Hondo and Pindi skeletal samples are almost certainly ancestral Tewa-Tano. Pecos, which for a long time was believed to be ancestral Towa, was instead possibly a Tewa or Tano pueblo. San Cristobal is a historically documented Tano site, an affiliation supported by archaeological evidence and consistent with the site's location in the middle of historic Tano territory. Unfortunately, no cranial samples from ancestral Keres sites were available for this analysis.

Kuaua, Pottery Mound, and Tijeras Pueblo lie within historically documented Southern Tiwa territory. The ethnolinguistic identification of the latter two rests partially on Mera's 1949 survey work. Hawikuh and Halona were late prehistoric to early historic Zuni villages that were visited by the Spaniards (Hodge 1907), and Awatovi was an important, historically documented Hopi village.

Three sites were temporally earlier than the others: Arroyo Hondo, Pindi, and Tijeras Pueblo. A number of other sites were founded as early as these three, but most were not abandoned until after Spanish contact in A.D. 1540. The populations of the earlier and later villages probably had an ancestor-descendant relationship; when Pindi and Arroyo Hondo were abandoned, their inhabitants presumably joined other late prehistoric Tewa-Tano pueblos. It would be of interest to see whether biological distance measures reflect this ancestor-descendant relationship. Another question of interest is whether contemporaneously occupied villages thought to be affiliated with a given tribe are more closely related to one another than to pueblos affiliated with other ethnolinguistic groups. In other words, is there any biological reality to the tribal divisions documented by the Spanish chroniclers and still observed today?

RESULTS

Table 36 gives the incidence of the 20 discrete traits in the 14 archaeological skeletal samples included in the study. Table 37 is the matrix of the mean measures of divergence between each pair of popu-

Appendix G

TABLE 36.
The incidence of the 20 discrete cranial traits in the 14 archaeological samples.
(Each number expresses the ratio of the skulls exhibiting a particular trait to the total number of skulls in the sample.)

	Arroyo Hondo	Puye	Pecos	Pecos Mission	San Cristobal	Pindi	Sapawe	Tijeras Pueblo	Kuaua	Pottery Mound	Giusewa	Awatovi	Hawikuh	Halona
Highest nuchal line present	.12	.076	.188	.10	.086	.118	.143	.00	.167	.167	.103	.097	.077	.188
Ossicle at lambda	.455	.51	.571	.15	.433	.526	.583	.188	.533	.60	.485	.613	.44	.563
Parietal foramen present	.864	.895	.895	.905	.941	.813	.91	.813	1.00	.80	.976	.906	.808	.938
Bregmatic bone present	.00	.014	.00	.043	.029	.067	.05	.00	.00	.04	.00	.053	.00	.00
Metopism	.00	.00	.00	.00	.025	.00	.00	.00	.034	.087	.00	.00	.00	.00
Epipteric bones present	.261	.25	.211	.20	.345	.214	.529	.125	.267	.158	.32	.296	.207	.125
Fronto—temporal articulation	.00	.032	.048	.00	.034	.00	.00	.00	.00	.00	.00	.00	.02	.00
Ossicle at asterion	.524	.70	.40	.455	.606	.533	.87	.571	.583	.619	.607	.895	.529	.50
Foramen of Huschke present	.156	.417	.158	.227	.351	.261	.222	.167	.184	.088	.341	.31	.50	.353
Exsutural mastoid foramen extant	.656	.824	.95	.588	.758	.714	.696	.364	.75	.842	.777	.84	.811	.647
Mastoid foramen absent	.032	.00	.00	.10	.031	.00	.00	.077	.75	.105	.00	.042	.019	.00
Patent posterior condylar canal	1.00	.984	.692	.857	.897	1.00	1.00	.833	.75	.857	1.00	.882	.936	.882
Condylar facet double	.00	.068	.00	.00	.00	.00	.077	.00	.00	.063	.087	.055	.00	.00
Precondylar tubercle present	.286	.237	.25	.308	.154	.00	.00	.167	.071	.353	.227	.158	.23	.176
Double anterior condylar canal	.185	.233	.25	.308	.259	.182	.33	.154	.389	.389	.783	.409	.208	.176
Accessory lesser palatine foramen present	.84	.923	.80	.867	.90	.692	.842	.944	.846	1.00	.966	.92	1.00	1.00
Zygomatic—facial foramen present	1.00	.971	1.00	1.00	.971	1.00	1.00	.875	.97	.875	.901	1.00	1.00	1.00
Supra-orbital foramen open	.759	.585	.75	.565	.821	.474	.778	.647	.765	.774	.675	.711	.732	.812
Frontal foramen or notch present	.666	.861	.95	.957	.868	.722	.84	.722	.853	.806	.895	.919	.857	1.00
Anterior ethmoid foramen exsutural	.269	.302	.429	.222	.414	.385	.375	.00	.217	.50	.31	.13	.288	.412

177

TABLE 37.

The matrix of mean measures of divergence for the 14 skeletal series.

Mean Number of Skulls Classified per Variate		Zuni		Hopi	Towa	Southern Tiwa					Tewa - Tano			
		Halona	Hawikuh	Awatovi	Giusewa	Pottery Mound	Kuaua	Tijeras Pueblo	Pecos Mission	Pecos	Sapawe	San Cristobal	Pindi	Puye
17	Halona	.0000*												
53	Hawikuh	.0557												
28	Awatovi	.1185	.0689											
32	Giusewa	.0913	.0461	.0653										
22	Pottery Mound	.0271	.0971	.0848	.0859									
23	Kuaua	.1695	.0879	.0363	.0770	.0893								
15	Tijeras Pueblo	.0384	.1443	.1678	.2620	.2223	.1962							
18	Pecos Mission	.0145	.0506	.0645	.1303	.1106	.0551	.0441						
18	Pecos	.1378	.0604	.0798	.1621	.0895	.0095	.1708	.0491					
21	Sapawe	.0171	.1651	.0301	.1015	.1901	.0838	.1904	.1737	.1712				
32	San Cristobal	.1278	.0179	.0290	.0819	.0508	.0349	.1458	.0173	.0130	.0577			
16	Pindi	.0562	.1230	.0951	.1671	.2074	.0892	.1762	.0912	.1026	.0032	.0481		
63	Puye		.0284	.0487	.0329	.1038	.0294	.1822	.0730	.0703	.0659	.0210	.0638	
27	Arroyo Hondo	.0880	.0452	.0805	.1135	.1015	.0671	.0998	.0359	.1056	.1109	.0370	.0289	.0426

*The variance due to sampling error is larger than the sum of the squared absolute differences between each pair of transformed measurements divided by the number of discrete traits measured for the two populations. This would result in a negative biological distance estimate.

lations. A small mean measure of divergence indicates high genetic similarity. The mean number of skulls classified per variate is different from the number of skulls studied (see Table 35) because not all skulls could be scored for all 20 variates.

The analysis of discrete cranial traits indicates that the Arroyo Hondo skeletal series is genetically similar to other Tewa-Tano samples: Pindi (.0289), San Cristobal (.0370), and Puye (.0426). Arroyo Hondo is also genetically similar to the historic Pecos Mission skeletal series (.0359), a somewhat surprising observation since the prehistoric Pecos sample is very dissimilar to Arroyo Hondo (.1056). The Pindi skeletal sample is also most closely aligned genetically with other Tewa and Tano samples: Sapawe (.0032), San Cristobal (.0481), and Puye (.0638), in addition to Arroyo Hondo.

No similar, simple generalization can be made for the other Tewa-Tano skeletal samples or those of the other ethnolinguistic groups. In fact, some of the results go against known southwestern culture history and extant Puebloan tribal divisions. For instance, prehistoric Pecos is more similar to the Southern Tiwa Kuaua sample and the ancestral Zuni sample of Halona than to Pecos Mission. Tijeras Pueblo, supposedly ancestral to the Southern Tiwa, is biologically very dissimilar to Southern Tiwa populations included in the analysis (Kuaua and Pottery Mound).

DISCUSSION

Clearly, some results do not support the classic anthropological view of the tribe (Romney 1957) in which a correlation between ethnolinguistic classification and genetics is expected. More recent work by physical anthropologists and biologists working with human populations has demonstrated that random genetic drift operates in small villages to create remarkable variability between villages within the same tribe. The results support this latter view.

Another problem may result from taking 14 samples and comparing each of them with the other 13, which produces 91 pairs of comparisons that supposedly reflect biological distance. We do not know how discrete cranial traits are inherited, and there may be a limit to the number of related populations that can be included and adequately summarized by a matrix of statistics. A certain percentage of seemingly closely related pairwise comparisons might be expected due to chance or sampling errors. In addition, this biological similarity analysis may not be fine-grained enough to reflect adequately the effects of common origin and intratribal, intervillage marriage, which act to counter the much larger effects of random genetic drift. Skeletal series from Hopi, Zuni, Towa, Tiwa, and Tewa-Tano villages scattered over 6,000 square miles and spanning 600 years of evolution are included, with only one or a few villages to represent each tribal group. It is difficult to compare intratribal, intervillage similarity and intertribal, intervillage biological similarity with the available skeletal series.

A finer-grained study might center on Tewa-Tano biological similarities and contrast these with a nearby tribal group such as the Towa. Table 38 lists the measures of divergence for the four ethnolinguistically related Tewa-Tano skeletal series and for the Towa series from Guisewa. There is a significant difference between the mean Towa-Tewa and Towa-Tano distance coefficients and the Tewa-Tano intervillage, intratribal coefficients. (Although one cannot necessarily equate biological significance with statistical significance, the t-test is significant at the .025 level.) The biological similarity among the Tewa-Tano villages and their dissimilarity to the spatially adjoining Towa village argue strongly for less intervillage, intratribal genetic variability than intervillage, intertribal variability.

Based on multivariate analysis of discrete cranial traits, the Arroyo Hondo skeletal series appears to be genetically similar to other probable ancestral Tewa and Tano skeletal series. This conclusion supports the archaeological evidence suggesting that Puye, Pindi, Arroyo Hondo, Sapawe, and other populations with ceramically and architecturally similar traditions form a cultural continuum that ends in historic Tewa-Tano villages.

TABLE 38.
The matrix of mean measure of divergence for Towa and Tewa-Tano skeletal series.

	Giusewa	Sapawe	Pindi	Puye	Arroyo Hondo
Sapawe	.1015				
Pindi	.1671	.0032			
Puye	.0329	.0659	.0638		
Arroyo Hondo	.1135	.1109	.0289	.0426	
San Cristobal	.0819	.0577	.0481	.0210	.0370

Appendix G

ACKNOWLEDGMENTS

The University of New Mexico, Peabody Museum, American Museum of Natural History, School of American Research, State Museum of New Mexico, Chicago Field Museum of Natural History, and Smithsonian Institution allowed access to their collections. William W. Howells, Richard W. Lang, and Ann M. Palkovich are thanked for their reviews of early drafts of this paper.

References

ABERLE, S. D.
1932   "Child Mortality Among Pueblo Indians," *American Journal of Physical Anthropology* 16:339–49.

ACSÁDI, G. Y., AND J. NEMESKÉRI
1970   *History of Human Life Span and Mortality* (Budapest: Akademiai Kiado).

AEGERTER, ERNEST, AND JOHN KIRKPATRICK
1968   *Orthopedic Diseases*, 3d ed. (Philadelphia: W. B. Saunders, Co.).

ANDERSON, D. L., G. W. THOMPSON, AND F. POPOVICH
1976   "Age of Attainment of Mineralization Stages of the Permanent Dentition," *Journal of Forensic Sciences* 21:191–200.

ANGEL, J. LAWRENCE
1966   Quoted in "Population Distances: Biological, Linguistic, Geographical, and Environmental," W. W. Howells, *Current Anthropology* 7:531–40.
1971   *The People of Lerna* (Washington, D. C.: Smithsonian Institution Press).

ASCH, DAVID
1976   *The Middle Woodland Population of the Lower Illinois Valley: A Study in Paleodemographic Methods*, Northwestern Archeological Program Scientific Papers, no. 1 (Evanston, Illinois: Northwestern University).

BANNISTER, BRYANT, JOHN W. HANNAH, AND WILLIAM J. ROBINSON
1970   *Tree-Ring Dates from New Mexico M-N, S, Z–Southwestern New Mexico Area*, Laboratory of Tree-Ring Research (Tucson: University of Arizona).

183

BENNETT, KENNETH
1973a   "On the Estimation of Some Demographic Characteristics on a Prehistoric
        Population from the American Southwest," *American Journal of Physical
        Anthropology* 39:223–32.
1973b   *The Indians of Point of Pines, Arizona: A Comparative Study of Their
        Physical Characteristics*, University of Arizona Anthropological Papers,
        no. 23 (Tucson).

BERRY, A. CAROLINE
1974   "The Use of Non-Metrical Variations of the Cranium in the Study of
        Scandinavian Population Movements," *American Journal of Physical An-
        thropology* 40:345–58.

BERRY, A. CAROLINE, AND R. J. BERRY
1967   "Epigenetic Variation in the Human Crania," *Journal of Anatomy*
        101:361–79.

BERRY, R. J.
1968   "Biology of Non-Metrical Variation in Mice and Men," in *The Skeletal
        Biology of Earlier Human Populations*, Symposia of the Society for the
        Study of Human Biology no. 8 (London: Taylor & Francis, Ltd.).

BIELICKI, TADEUSZ
1962   "Some Possibilities for Estimating Inter-Population Relationship on the
        Basis of Continuous Traits," *Current Anthropology* 3:3–46.

BINFORD, LEWIS
1971   "Mortuary Practices: Their Study and Their Potential," in *Approaches to
        the Social Dimensions of Mortuary Practices*, ed. James A. Brown, Society
        for American Archaeology Memoir no. 25 (Washington, D. C.).

BLALOCK, HUBERT
1972   *Social Statistics*, 2d ed. (New York: McGraw-Hill).

BREATHNACH, A. S.
1965   *Frazer's Anatomy of the Human Skeleton* (London: J. & A. Churchill).

BROTHWELL, DON
1972   *Digging Up Bones*, 2d ed. (London: British Museum).

BROWN, JAMES A. (ED.)
1971   *Approaches to the Social Dimension of Mortuary Practices*, Society for
        American Archaeology Memoir no. 25 (Washington, D.C.).

CARLSON, DAVID, GEORGE ARMELAGOS, AND DENNIS VAN GERVAN
1974   "Factors Affecting the Etiology of Cribra Orbitalia in Prehistoric Nubia,"
        Journal of Human Evolution 3:405–10.

CASTAÑEDA, PEDRO DE
1940   "Castañeda's History of the Coronado Expedition," in *Narratives of the*

References

                Coronado Expedition, 1540–1542, ed. and trans. George P. Hammond and Agapito Rey (Albuquerque: University of New Mexico Press).

CAVALLI-SFORZA, LUIGI
1969   "Genetic Drift in an Italian Population," *Scientific American* 221:30–37.

CLARK, GEOFFREY A.
1969   "A Preliminary Analysis of Burial Clusters at the Grasshopper Site, East Central Arizona," *The Kiva* 35:1–30.

CORRUCCINI, ROBERT
1972   "The Biological Relationships of Some Prehistoric and Historic Pueblo Populations," *American Journal of Physical Anthropology* 37:373–88.
1974   "An Examination of the Meaning of Cranial Discrete Traits for Human Skeletal Biological Studies," *American Journal of Physical Anthropology* 40:425–45.

DEAN, JEFFREY S., AND WILLIAM J. ROBINSON
1977   *Dendroclimatic Variability in the American Southwest, A.D. 680 to 1970*, Laboratory of Tree-Ring Research, Report to National Park Service (Tucson: University of Arizona).

DENNIS, WAYNE
1940   *The Hopi Child* (New York: Appleton-Century Co.).

DUBOS, RENE
1965   *Man Adapting* (New Haven: Yale University Press).

DWIGHT, THOMAS
1904–05 "The Size of the Articular Surfaces of the Long Bones as Characteristic of Sex: An Anthropological Study," *American Journal of Anatomy* 4:19–31.

EGGAN, FRED
1950   *Social Organization of the Western Pueblos* (Chicago: University of Chicago Press).

ELLIS, FLORENCE HAWLEY
1968   "An Interpretation of Prehistoric Death Customs in Terms of Modern Southwestern Parallels," in *Collected Papers in Honor of Lyndon Lane Hargrave*, Papers of the Archeological Society of New Mexico, no. 1 (Santa Fe: Museum of New Mexico Press).

EL-NAJJAR, MAHMOUD
1974   "People of Canyon de Chelly: A Study of Their Biology and Culture," (Ph.D. diss., Arizona State University).
1977   "Maize, Malaria, and the Anemias in the Pre-Columbian New World," in *Yearbook of Physical Anthropology, 1976* 20:329–37.

EL-NAJJAR, MAHMOUD, B. LOZOFF, AND D. RYAN
1975   "The Paleo-Epidemiology of Porotic Hyperostosis in the American South-

west: Radiological and Ecological Considerations," *American Journal of Roentgenology, Radium Therapy, and Nuclear Medicine* 25:918–24.

EL-NAJJAR, MAHMOUD, D. RYAN, C. TURNER, AND B. LOZOFF
1976   "The Etiology of Porotic Hyperostosis among the Prehistoric and Historic Anasazi Indians of Southwestern United States," *American Journal of Physical Anthropology* 44:477–88.

FLECKER, H.
1942   "Time of Appearance and Fusion of Ossification Centers as Observed by Roentgenographic Methods," *American Journal of Roentgenology, Radium Therapy and Nuclear Medicine* 47:97–159.

FRANCIS, G. C., AND P. P. WERLE
1939   "The Appearance of Centers of Ossification from Birth to 5 Years," *American Journal of Physical Anthropology* 24:273–99.

GARN, STANLEY
1966   "Nutrition in Physical Anthropology," *American Journal of Physical Anthropology* 24:289–92.

GENOVÉS, SANTIAGO
1967   "Proportionality of the Long Bones and Their Relation to Stature Among Mesoamericans," *American Journal of Physical Anthropology* 26:67–78.

GILBERT, B. MILES, AND THOMAS McKERN
1971   "A Method of Aging the Female Os Pubis," *American Journal of Physical Anthropology* 38:31–38.

GOLDSTEIN, MARCUS
1969   "Human Paleopathology and Some Diseases in Living Primitive Societies: A Review of the Recent Literature," *American Journal of Physical Anthropology* 31:285–94.

GORDON, J. E., J. B. WYON, AND W. ASCOLI
1967   "The Second Year Death Rate in Less Developed Countries," *American Journal of Medical Science* 254:357–80.

GOSS, CHARLES MAYO (ED.)
1966   *Gray's Anatomy*, 28th ed. (Philadelphia: Lea and Febiger).

HEGLAR, ROGER
1974   "The Prehistoric Population of Cochiti and Selected Inter-Population Biological Comparisons," (Ph.D. diss., University of Michigan).

HENGEN, O. P.
1971   "Cribra Orbitalia: Pathogenesis and Probable Etiology," *Homo* 22:57–75.

HODGE, FREDERICK WEBB (ED.)
1907   *Handbook of American Indians North of Mexico*, parts 1 and 2, Bureau of American Ethnology Bulletin no. 30 (Washington, D. C.).

References

HOOTON, E. A.
1930   *The Indians of Pecos Pueblo* (New Haven: Yale University Press, Phillips Academy).

JAFFE, H. L.
1972   *Metabolic, Degenerative and Inflammatory Disease of Bones and Joints* (Philadelphia: Lea and Febiger).

JARCHO, S., N. SIMON, AND H. L. JAFFE
1965   "Symmetrical Osteoporosis (Spongy Hyperostosis) in a Prehistoric Skull from New Mexico," *El Palacio* 72:26–30.

JOHNSTON, E. F.
1961   "Sequence of Epiphyseal Union in a Prehistoric Kentucky Population from Indian Knoll," *Human Biology* 33:66–81.
1962   "Growth of Long Bones of Infants and Young Children at Indian Knoll," *American Journal of Physical Anthropology* 20:249–54.

KEPP, D. J.
1972   "Preliminary Burial Report, Arroyo Hondo Project," unpublished ms. (Santa Fe: School of American Research).

KERLEY, ELLIS
1970   "Estimation of Skeletal Age: After About Age 30," in *Personal Identification in Mass Disasters*, ed. T. Dale Stewart (Washington, D. C.: Smithsonian Institution Press).

KIDDER, ALFRED
1958   *Pecos, New Mexico: Archeological Notes* (New Haven: Yale University Press).

KROGMAN, W. M.
1962   *The Human Skeleton in Forensic Medicine* (Springfield, Illinois: Charles C. Thomas, Publishers).

KRONFELD, RUDOLF
1935   "Development and Calcification of the Human Deciduous and Permanent Dentition," *The Bur* 35:18–25.

KRZYWICKI, LUDWIK
1934   *Primitive Society and Its Vital Statistics* (London: Macmillian and Co. Publishers).

KUNITZ, STEPHEN, AND ROBERT EULER
1972   *Aspects of Southwestern Paleoepidemiology*, Prescott College Press Anthropological Reports, no. 2 (Prescott, Arizona).

LALLO, JOHN, GEORGE ARMELAGOS, AND ROBERT MENSFORTH
1977   "The Role of Diet, Disease, and Physiology in the Origin of Porotic Hyperostosis," *Human Biology* 49:471–83.

187

LAMBERT, MARJORIE
1954   *Paa-ko, Archeological Chronicle of an Indian Village in North Central New Mexico*, parts I-IV, School of American Research Monograph no. 19 (Santa Fe).

LANG, RICHARD W.
n.d.   "Arroyo Hondo Ceramics Analysis," unpublished ms. (Santa Fe: School of American Research).

LANGE, CHARLES
1968   *The Cochiti Dam Archeological Salvage Project*, Museum Records no. 6 (Santa Fe: Museum of New Mexico).

LONGACRE, WILLIAM
1976   "Population Dynamics at the Grasshopper Pueblo, Arizona," in *Demographic Anthropology: Quantitative Approaches*, ed. Ezra Zubrow (Albuquerque: University of New Mexico Press, School of American Research Advanced Seminar Series).

LOVEJOY, C. OWEN
1971   "Methods for the Detection of Census Error in Palaeodemography," *American Anthropologist* 73:101–109.

LOVEJOY, C. OWEN, RICHARD MEINDL, THOMAS PRYZBECK, THOMAS BARTON, KINGSBURY HEIPLE, AND DAVID KNOTTING
1977   "Paleodemography of the Libben Site, Ottawa County, Ohio," *Science* 198:291–93.

LUMPKIN, C. K.
1976   "A Multivariate Craniometric Analysis of Selected Southwestern Archaeological Populations" (Ph.D. diss., University of New Mexico).

MACKAY, R. HUGO
1961   *Skeletal Maturation Chart* (Rochester, New York: Eastman-Kodak Co.).

MACKEY, JAMES
1977   "A Multivariate, Osteological Approach to Towa Culture History," *American Journal of Physical Anthropology* 46:477–82.

MALTBY, J. R. D.
1917–18 "Some Indices and Measurements of the Modern Femur," *Journal of Anatomy* 52:363–82.

McKERN, THOMAS
1970   "Estimation of Skeletal Age: From Puberty to About 30 Years of Age," in *Personal Identification in Mass Disasters*, ed. T. Dale Stewart (Washington, D. C.: Smithsonian Institution Press).

McKERN, THOMAS W., AND T. DALE STEWART
1957   *Skeletal Age Changes in Young American Males, Analyzed from the Stand-*

point of Age Identification, Technical Report EP-45, Environmental Protection Research Division, Quartermaster Research and Development Center, U. S. Army (Natick, Mass.).

MEINDL, RICHARD, AND ALAN SWEDLUND
1977   "Secular Trends in Mortality in the Connecticut Valley, 1700–1850," *Human Biology* 49:389–414.

MENSFORTH, ROBERT, C. OWEN LOVEJOY, JOHN LALLO, AND GEORGE ARMELAGOS
1978   "The Role of Constitutional Factors, Diet, and Infectious Disease in the Etiology of Porotic Hyperostosis and Periosteal Reactions in Prehistoric Infants and Children," *Medical Anthropology* 2:1–59.

MERA, H. P.
1934   *A Survey of the Biscuit Ware Area in Northern New Mexico*, Museum of New Mexico Laboratory of Anthropology Technical Series Bulletin no. 6 (Santa Fe).
1940   *Population Changes in the Rio Grande Glaze Paint Area*, Museum of New Mexico Laboratory of Anthropology Technical Series Bulletin no. 9 (Santa Fe).

MILES, JAMES
1966   "Diseases Encountered at Mesa Verde, Colorado: II. Evidences of Disease," in *Human Paleopathology*, ed. Saul Jarcho (New Haven: Yale University Press).

MODI, J. P.
1957   *Medical Jurisprudence and Toxicology*, 12th ed. (Bombay: Tripathi Private, Ltd.).

MOORE, JAMES, ALAN SWEDLUND, AND GEORGE ARMELAGOS
1975   "The Use of Life Tables in Paleodemography," in *Population Studies in Archaeology and Biological Anthropology: A Symposium*, ed. Alan Swedlund, Society for American Archaeology Memoir no. 30 (Washington, D. C.).

MOORREES, COENRAAD, ELIZABETH FANNING, AND EDWARD HUNT
1963a   "Formation and Resorption of Three Deciduous Teeth in Children," *American Journal of Physical Anthropology* 21:205–13.
1963b   "Age Variation of Formation Stages for Ten Permanent Teeth," *Journal of Dental Research* 42:1,490–1,502.

MORSE, DAN
1969   *Ancient Disease in the Midwest*, Reports of Investigation, no. 15 (Springfield, Ill.: Illinois State Museum).

NEEL, JAMES V., AND RICHARD H. WARD
1970   "Village and Tribal Genetic Distances Among American Indians, and the Possible Implications for Human Evolution," *Proceedings, National Academy of Sciences* 65:323–30.

NELSON, NELS C.
1915   "Pueblos Arroyo Hondo," unpublished ms. (American Museum of Natural History).

ORTIZ, ALFONSO
1969   *The Tewa World* (Chicago: University of Chicago Press).

ORTNER, DONALD
1975   "Porotic Hyperostosis of the Skull in Metabolic Disease," paper presented at American Association of Physical Anthropologists Annual Meeting.

PALKOVICH, ANN M.
1978   "A Model of the Dimensions of Mortality and Its Application to Paleodemography" (Ph.D. diss., Northwestern University).

PARSONS, ELSIE CLEWS
1929   *The Social Organization of the Tewa, New Mexico*, American Anthropological Association Memoir no. 36 (Menasha, Wis.).
1939   *Pueblo Indian Religion* (Chicago: University of Chicago Press).

PARSONS, F. G.
1914–15 "The Characters of the English Thigh Bone, Part II: The Difficulty of Sexing," *Journal of Anatomy and Physiology* 49:235–61.

PEARSON, KARL
1917–18 A *Study of the Long Bones of the English Skeleton, I. Femur*, Draper's Co. Research Memoir, University of London Biometric Series X (London: Cambridge University Press).

PHENICE, T. W.
1969   "A Newly Developed Visual Method of Sexing the Os Pubis," *American Journal of Physical Anthropology* 30:297–301.

PUFFER, RUTH, AND CARLOS SERRANO
1973   *Patterns of Mortality in Childhood*, Pan American Health Organization Scientific Publication no. 22 (Washington, D. C.).

REDFIELD, ALAN
1970   "A New Aid to Aging Immature Skeletons: Development of the Occipital Bone," *American Journal of Physical Anthropology* 33:207–20.

REED, ERIK
1966   "The 14th Century Population of the Galisteo Basin: Skeletal Remains and Burial Methods," unpublished ms. (Santa Fe: Laboratory of Anthropology).
1967   "Human Skeletal Material from the Gran Quivira District," unpublished ms. (Santa Fe: Laboratory of Anthropology).

RHOADS, JOHN G., AND JONATHAN S. FRIEDLAENDER
1975   "Language Boundaries and Biological Differentiation on Bougainville: Multivariate Analysis of Variance," *Proceedings, National Academy of Sciences* 65:323–30.

References

ROBINSON, WILLIAM J., JOHN W. HANNAH, AND BRUCE G. HARRILL
1972   *Tree-Ring Dates from New Mexico I, O, U*, Laboratory of Tree-Ring Research (Tucson: University of Arizona).

ROBINSON, WILLIAM J., BRUCE G. HARRILL, AND RICHARD L. WARREN
1973   *Tree-Ring Dates from New Mexico J-K, P, V*, Laboratory of Tree-Ring Research (Tucson: University of Arizona).

ROGERS, SPENCER
1954   *The Physical Type of the Paa-ko Population*, part VI, School of American Research Monograph no. 19 (Santa Fe).

ROMNEY, A. KIMBALL
1957   "The Genetic Model and Uto-Aztecan Time Perspective," *Davidson Journal of Anthropology* 3:35–41.

ROSE, MARTIN R., JEFFREY S. DEAN, AND WILLIAM J. ROBINSON
1979   *"Past Climate of Arroyo Hondo Reconstructed from Tree Rings,"* unpublished ms. (Santa Fe: School of American Research).

ROYCHOUDHURY, A. K.
1975   "Genetic Distance and Gene Diversity Among Linguistically Different Tribes of Mexican Indians," *American Journal of Physical Anthropology* 42:449–54.

SAXE, ARTHUR
1970   "Social Dimensions of Mortuary Practices" (Ph.D. diss., University of Michigan).

SCHOENWETTER, JAMES, AND ALFRED E. DITTERT, JR.
1968   "An Ecological Interpretation of Anasazi Settlement Patterns," in *Anthropological Archeology in the Americas*, ed. Betty J. Meggers (Washington, D. C.: The Anthropological Society of Washington).

SCHORSCH, RUSSELL L. G.
1956   "Pottery Mound: A Pueblo IV Site in West Central New Mexico—The Physical Anthropology of Pottery Mound" (M.A. thesis, University of New Mexico).

SCHOUR, I., AND M. MASSLER
1941   "The Development of the Human Dentition," *Journal of the American Dental Association* 28:1,153–60.

SCHWARTZ, DOUGLAS
1970   "Cultural and Ecological Ramifications of Population Growth," unpublished research proposal submitted to the National Science Foundation (Santa Fe: School of American Research).

SIEGEL, SIDNEY
1956   *Nonparametric Statistics* (New York: McGraw-Hill).

191

SMILEY, TERAH L.
1951   A *Summary of Tree-Ring Dates from Some Southwestern Archaeological Sites*, University of Arizona Bulletin no. 22 (Tucson).

STALLINGS, W. S.
1937   *Southwestern Dated Ruins: I*, Tree-Ring Bulletin of the University of Arizona, vol. 4, no. 2, pp. 3–5 (Tucson).

STEINBOCK, R. TED
1976   *Paleopathological Diagnosis and Interpretation* (Springfield, Illinois: Charles C. Thomas, Publishers).

STEVENSON, P. H.
1924   "Age Order of Epiphyseal Union in Man," *American Journal of Physical Anthropology* 7:53–93.

STEWART, T. DALE
1958   "The Rate of Development of Vertebral Osteoarthritis in American Males and Its Significance in Skeletal Identification," *The Leech* 28:144–51.

STINI, W. A.
1973   "Adaptive Strategies of Human Population Under Nutritional Stress," paper presented at the IXth International Congress of Anthropological and Ethnological Sciences (Chicago).

STUBBS, STANLEY, AND W. S. STALLINGS, JR.
1953   *The Excavation of Pindi, New Mexico*, School of American Research Monograph no. 18 (Santa Fe).

SWEDLUND, ALAN, AND GEORGE ARMELAGOS
1969   "Une Recherche en Paléo-Démographie: la Nubie Soudanaise," *Annales-Economies-Societies-Civilizations* 6:1,287–98.

TELKKA, A.
1950   "On Prediction of Human Stature from the Long Bones," *Acta Anatomica* 9:103–17.

THIEME, F. P., AND W. J. SCHULL
1957   "Sex Determination from the Skeleton," *Human Biology* 29:242–73.

TODD, T. W.
1920   "Age Changes in the Pubic Bone, Part I," *American Journal of Physical Anthropology* 3:285–334.
1921   "Age Changes in the Pubic Bone, Parts II-IV," *American Journal of Physical Anthropology* 4:1–70.
1923   "Age Changes in the Pubic Symphysis VII: The Anthropoid Strain in Human Pubic Symphysis of the Third Decade," *Journal of Anatomy* 57:274–94.

TODD, T. W., AND J. D'ERRICO
1928   "The Clavicular Epiphyses," *American Journal of Anatomy* 41:25–50.

References

TODD, T. W., AND D. W. LYON
1924   "Endocranial Suture Closure, Its Progress and Age Relationship, Part I: Adult Males of White Stock," *American Journal of Physical Anthropology* 7:325–84.
1925   "Cranial Suture Closure, Its Progress and Age Relationship, Part II: Ecto-cranial Closure in Adult Males of White Stock." *American Journal of Physical Anthropology* 8:23–71.

UBELAKER, DOUGLAS
1974   *Reconstruction of Demographic Profiles from Ossuary Skeletal Samples: A Case Study from the Tidewater Potomac,* Smithsonian Contributions to Anthropology, no. 18 (Washington, D. C.).
1978   *Human Skeletal Remains: Excavation, Analysis, Interpretation* (Chicago: Aldine Publishing Co.).

VALLOIS, HENRI
1960   "Vital Statistics in Prehistoric Population as Determined from Archeological Data," in *The Application of Quantitative Methods in Archaeology,* ed. Robert Heizer and Sherburne Cook, Viking Fund Publications in Anthropology, no. 28 (Chicago: Quadrangle Books).
1965   "Anthropometric Techniques," *Current Anthropology* 6:127–43.

WALKER, HELEN, AND JOSEPH LEV
1953   *Statistical Inference* (New York: Holt, Rinehart and Winston).

WASHBURN, S. L.
1948   "Sex Differences in the Pubic Bone," *American Journal of Physical Anthropology* 6:199–207.

WEISS, KENNETH
1973   *Demographic Models for Anthropology,* Memoirs of the Society for American Archaeology no. 27 (Washington, D. C.).
1976   "Demographic Theory and Anthropological Inference," *Annual Review of Anthropology* 5:351–81.

WENDORF, FRED, AND ERIK REED
1955   "An Alternative Reconstruction of Northern Rio Grande Prehistory," *El Palacio* 62:131–73.

WETTERSTROM, WILMA
1976   "The Effects of Nutrition on Population Size at Pueblo Arroyo Hondo," (Ph.D. diss., University of Michigan).

WHITE, LESLIE
1942   *The Pueblo of Santa Ana, New Mexico,* American Anthropological Association Memoir no. 60 (Menasha, Wis.).
1962   *The Pueblo of Sia, New Mexico,* Bureau of American Ethnology Bulletin no. 184 (Washington, D. C.).

193

WILLS, V. G., AND J. C. WATERLOO
1958   "The Death Rate in Age Group 1–4 Years as an Index of Malnutrition,"
          Journal of Tropical Pediatrics 3:167–70.

ZAINO, EDWARD
1967   "Symmetrical Osteoporosis, A Sign of Severe Anemia in the Prehistoric
          Pueblo Indians of the Southwest," in *Miscellaneous Papers in Paleopathology:
          I*, ed. William Wade, Museum of Northern Arizona Technical Series no.
          7 (Flagstaff).
1968   "Elemental Bone Iron in the Anasazi Indians," *American Journal of Physi-
          cal Anthropology* 29:433–35.